CREATOR

SUSTAINER

GOD

PROTECTOR

THE TREE THAT FELL TO THE WEST

Autobiography of a Sufi

by

M. R. BAWA MUHAIYADDEEN

The Fellowship Press
Philadelphia, PA

Library of Congress Cataloging-in-Publication Data

Muhaiyaddeen, M. R. Bawa.
    The tree that fell to the west : autobiography of a Sufi / M. R. Bawa Muhaiyaddeen.
        p.   cm.
    ISBN 0-914390-67-8
    1. Muhaiyaddeen, M. R. Bawa. 2. Sufis--Biography. I. Title.

BP80.M778A3 2003
297.4'092--dc21
    [B]   2003049237

Printed in the United States of America
by THE FELLOWSHIP PRESS
The Bawa Muhaiyaddeen Fellowship
First Printing

Muhammad Raheem Bawa Muhaiyaddeen ﵁

TABLE OF CONTENTS

EDITOR'S NOTE   *ix*

INTRODUCTION   *xi*

1. THE WAY OF THE WORLD   *1*

2. THE PATH OF DUTY   *15*

3. THE TREE THAT FELL TO THE WEST   *21*

4. BAWA MUHAIYADDEEN ☺ AS A YOUNG BOY   *25*

5. BAWA MUHAIYADDEEN ☺ THE KING   *31*

6. THE DIVINE ASSEMBLY   *41*

7. THE ROCKY MOUNTAIN   *49*

8. WHAT BAWA MUHAIYADDEEN ☺ HEARD WHILE IN MEDITATION   *61*

9. THE TRUE VALUE OF EXPERIENCE   *71*

10. LIFE IN THE JUNGLE   *75*

11. BAWA MUHAIYADDEEN ☺ AND THE ELEPHANTS   *81*

12. THE COW   *83*

13. BAWA MUHAIYADDEEN ☺ AND THE SNAKE   *85*

14. HOW BAWA MUHAIYADDEEN ☺ BECAME A BEGGAR   *89*

15. HOW BAWA MUHAIYADDEEN ☺ BECAME A BAKER   *99*

16. HOW BAWA MUHAIYADDEEN ☺ LOST HIS ANGER   *103*

17. ROUNDING   107

18. THE MEANING OF HIS NAME   111

19. ACCIDENTS   113

20. THE BOOK AND THE BOX   117

21. A TRIP TO KATHIRAKAMAM   121

22. A VISION AT THE GATES OF HELL   131

23. THE IMPORTANCE OF PRAYER   135

24. MEETING THE RASŪL ⊕   139

25. THE QUTB ⊕ ACTS AS A BUFFER TO EVIL   145

26. A JOURNEY FROM MEDINA TO BAGHDAD: HOW TO
     RECOGNIZE THE TRUTH   153

27. PROPHETS AND QUTBS   159

28. THE ANT MAN QUTB ⊕   163

29. THE MOSQUE   167

30. THE DISCIPLE MUST MERGE WITH THE GURU   173

31. A PRAYER FOR HIS CHILDREN   179

32. ONLY GOD HAS A HISTORY   187

GLOSSARY   191

Editor's Note

A'ūdhu billāhi minash-shaitānir-rajīm.
Bismillāhir-Rahmānir-Rahīm.

It is said that if all the trees in the world were made into pens and all the oceans were made into ink, one could never finish writing about the mysteries of God.

Indeed, one of God's great mysteries is the story of Muhammad Raheem Bawa Muhaiyaddeen ☺. Bawa Muhaiyaddeen ☺ was reluctant to speak of himself; his emphasis was that only God has a true history. He did, however, over a period of fourteen years, relate fragments of his story.

These stories touched our hearts and woke the gently sleeping seed of love and wonder within us. With this love we gathered together some of these fragments in an attempt to piece together this great journey of God's *Qutb* ☺.

In 1942 Bawa Muhaiyaddeen ☺ wrote in a book he titled *Guru Mani* that the fruits of the Tree of Wisdom which he had established in the East would fall in the West. Here, dear reader, is a tiny portion of some of these exquisite fruits.

As-salāmu 'alaikum, may peace be upon you all.

Rabia Miller

INTRODUCTION

Bismillāhir-Rahmānir-Rahīm.

Light: "Electromagnetic radiation that can be detected by the human eye. In terms of wavelength, electromagnetic radiation occurs over an extremely wide range, from gamma rays with a wavelength of 3 10-14 centimeter to long radio waves measured in millions of kilometers. In that spectrum the wavelengths visible to humans occupy a very small segment of this spectrum…"

If we possessed the full range of vision with which to see the entire spectrum how very different our perception of existence would be.

Similarly, if we were to gain full awareness of ourselves, full consciousness, we would perceive other beings, so unlike us in their makeup that we, the creatures of darkness, trapped in space and time, cannot register their existence with our earthbound senses. Beyond created matter, they live in the realm of divine light, existing within and consisting of, God's qualities. The prophets, the angels, the *qutbs,* the saints—all exist within and as the Light of Allah.

The 'face' of Allah is His Light, the Nūr Muhammad or Light Muhammad, through which Allah manifests all creation, from the refined paradise of His qualities all the way to creation of matter and darkness.

From time to time God assigns one of these beings which are of His aspect to take bodily form for the purpose of transmitting explanations of His truth to His creations born into this world. Over millions of years countless numbers have come, appeared on earth, and, under extreme duress and with great difficulty, given God's explanations, then disappeared again back into His formless Light. Always they have come with the same message: "The Creator is One. This is truth, His Oneness. This is reality; there is only One and God is that One." The languages, the names, change from culture to culture, the truth does not. There is the One who creates all else.

All else, that which human science measures, counts, and calculates, the space and time of it, is ultimately an illusion both within our minds and outside ourselves. Not real, not permanent, similar to a projection on a screen.

When an artist prepares to do an oil painting, first the prepared canvas is covered with a dark wash of paint as background then the subject is created from dark to light with shadows first then gradual layering of paint to the lightest applied last, an illusion of form created according to the artist's ability.

Creation, matter or form, is something like this. Earth, fire, water, air, ether, the paints of creation, the illusion masterfully and exquisitely done by the one true Artist, and within that illusion we perceive that we exist, the creatures of darkness, our bodies, thoughts, desires, attachments and beliefs—the limits of our perception. From Light we are born, but we live and die, never knowing the Artist, believing this world and ourselves to be the limits of reality.

Yet God with infinite mercy sends His messengers to tell us over and over again: No! What we think is not the truth. We are blind and deaf and dumb, sleeping soundly in our dreams in the darkness. His messengers tirelessly explain that there is a way to discover that truth which is reality, the One. The way is built into the heart, a hidden secret, and a point the revelation of which stretches even to eternity, and far beyond, transcending the senses and form.

To reveal this secret one must first believe that God does exist beyond the illusion. Then dedicate one's self exclusively to Him, yearn only to know Him, intend only to find Him, focus fiercely upon this intention, and surrender, surrender, surrender!

If one accomplishes complete surrender what will happen then is the disappearance of this earth world. First to go is sound. Silence. Then sight, gone. Awareness, remaining, perceives another sight which sees anywhere, anything intended is viewed within. This realm also disappears.

But then, oh then! All worldly existence forgotten, awareness awestruck and wide-awake:

The Explanation begins. Silent, yet a spoken word, the Qur'an recites itself, explaining that which you have never heard. Transfixed, awareness becomes that which is explained, as the explanation expands so does awareness, so fast, so exalted. Rising through realm upon realm of Wisdom's revelation, where formless beings exist as divine qualities.

Then, transported awareness hears, "There is no space or time! There is only one Thing, and I am That!" Then Light! Simultaneously Awareness becomes Voice becomes Light becomes One.

The final perception of awareness is becoming the Light. That which has ceased to exist cannot perceive the One. Only Allah can know Allah.

The explaining Voice is called Muhaiyaddeen or Wisdom, it explains all the mysteries of the divine realms to our astonished soul. The Messenger is God's Light, called Nūr or Light Muhammad. This Light is the 'edge' or 'face' of the One into which individuated awareness disappears. It is this Light through which all creation is created. God's Light shines forth, creation is. Follow the Light to its source and the One is. This One is Reality; it is The One. There is no other.

This book is about the 'history' of Muhaiyaddeen. Which Muhaiyaddeen should we speak of? I will tell a little about the one I know. In 1963, I experienced what is described above, quite suddenly. I had no previous conscious knowledge of any of it. It happened.

My consciousness eventually returned to a world seemingly devoid of any knowledge of this One. I quickly learned that to speak of it was not acceptable or wise; people merely thought I had lost my mind.

Not knowing what to do or where to turn I began to earnestly pray to that One: What am I to do here alone, a stranger in a strange land? Please send someone! Please send someone! For eight years I pled. I begged. I cried. Then in 1968, following awareness's inner instruction, I located his name: Muhammad Raheem Bawa Muhaiyaddeen. It was he! I was certain and, it was he! I never doubted for a second even though he was twelve thousand miles away and I had never heard of him.

It was he. Two more years of another kind of begging; please come, please come, this time with letters exchanged, promises made and in 1971 on October 11 at 4:45 p.m. Muhammad Raheem Bawa Muhaiyaddeen arrived in Philadelphia.

He spoke. I sat transfixed and openly stared at this miracle. Stunned. Every word he spoke was an exact description of the experience I had. To my perception he had manifested from that One and he spoke only of that One. I knew then and I know now that this was not an ordinary human being. This was an extraordinary being sent by God. Every word he said was true whether it was an explanation of God or an explanation of how the world worked or how the mind of man worked. Every example, every story ended in God and there were thousands of examples and stories and songs and discourses, all about the One.

Everything he saw he turned into an example; even the plastic trash bags we used in America to put out the garbage and the story would end in God. He spoke morning, noon and night. He sang beautiful glorious songs about and to God. When people came for the first time he would tell them everything about themselves. It was the 1970's and when 'gurus' came he would scold them severely for deceiving naive Americans for money. Begging him not to expose them (which he had just done), they would cry, shaking with fear and run away. Slowly the audience grew, mostly longtime spiritual searchers from the Philadelphia area. Word got around, someone very special is here. Come listen. For nine months we sat happily at his feet, soaking up whatever we could hold within ourselves.

Then he returned to Sri Lanka. Some of us followed, to Colombo, to Jaffna, to Perideniya, all places spoken of in this book. What we saw and experienced there could fill books also. We saw the thousands of desperately poor he fed and healed. We saw people possessed by demons, and I guarantee you demons are real; we saw things difficult to imagine, yet we saw them, and him, rising above it all, the only true human being I have ever seen. He taught Hindus in Jaffna, Muslims in Colombo, Christians and Jews in America, speaking Truth to their perspective, but it would all end in the One as the only reality.

Islam he defined as purity, Muhammad, the Light of the One. We learned new meanings for new languages, Tamil and Arabic. We learned, we studied, and we loved him.

He was love, caring for us in a way none of us had ever known and we thrived on the purity of that love and learned and grew as human beings. He taught us the same Truth that had been revealed through the ages by all the prophets: worship only the One God, care for all lives as you do your own.

The stories in this book may seem fantastic to some, confusing to some, spanning as they do a time frame of hundreds, even thousands of years, but please remember our sense of reality is linear, the realm of God's reality is not. The realm Muhaiyaddeen lives from is not subject to the time-space rules we experience, so I testify that whatever is said in this book is true.

We knew, lived with, and loved many of the people spoken of in these stories and they told us the stories also, such as the elephant story with Araby, Ameen and Dr. Ajwad. Most of these wonderful people have passed on and we sorely miss them.

There are further explanations I could give about him, things he told us here and there on very rare occasions, as he seldom spoke of himself, for, no matter how exceptional the creation, it is only God who is the exceptional One. A true human being, having known that One sees all else as insignificant—an ant man he called himself. A deeply overwhelming sense of humility comes from being in God's presence, what else could one feel? In the remembrance of God's Light, any awareness of one's self is an acute embarrassment.

What purpose or reason for existence could this earth world offer to someone like him? Why stay? It can be summed up in one word: Duty.

What duty? When one has experienced God and returned forged as one with God, changed and fully aware that all else is false, one must tell others. There is an impulse, a compulsion to do so, combined with compassion for all lives as they go about in ignorance of this glory. One must tell them; it is dedication, duty, and gratitude, for how could one leave His glorious story untold?

This is the work of the prophets and the *qutbs,* those true human beings, so different from us, who spend their every moment in conscious remembrance of that One. Their awareness stretches the full spectrum of God's Light, it comes from Allah to this world we live in, and extends back to Allah, the One.

Al-hamdu lillāh, all praise, all worship is due to God, the creator of all things. May Allah's peace forever be upon His beloved and most worthy servant Muhammad Raheem Bawa Muhaiyaddeen. *Āmīn.*

Carolyn Fatima Andrews
"Secretary"

1 | THE WAY OF THE WORLD

P recious jeweled lights of my eye, may God protect you. Many things happen during our lifetime my children, and I am thinking about something, something I experienced which I feel compelled to speak about now. There are many reasons why God has created us, and there is a period of time when we should try to understand these reasons, and to understand from this what our duties are and why we should carry them out. There might be many such explanations.

It had always been my intention to find out what my Father was like, to know who God was, to understand His nature. I wanted to discover some way to see Him and undertook to work hard at this with all the clarity of my wisdom. Now I am extremely old, but earlier, for long periods of time I searched and searched. With this searching I came to certain understandings, one of which I want to tell you now. There are certain things I can never disclose, some secrets I cannot reveal, but I can tell you some of my experiences. I started the search for my Father when I was still very young. I searched and searched and searched, trying hard to understand, yet all I learned concerned the world. I saw only the world, the gurus just taught me about the world. They would say, "If you do such and such you can reach God," and I would try it. I would practice with more earnestness and zeal than they did. Whatever they taught, whatever effort they made, I exerted myself a hundred times more.

They taught me miracles and mantras, magic and tricks, they taught me certain mental powers, but it so happened that I had to teach *them* what these things were all about. I had to expose the flaws in what they taught and say, "I did not come in search of this. I came to understand what my life is about, who my Father is, I came to read the story of my Father."

Then I left the gurus and went into the four religions. The leaders of these religions claimed that God existed only in their religion. I studied each of them. I studied hard, very hard, but the God I had within my wisdom was not to be found there. I became obsessed, absolutely obsessed to see my Father, and so I left and went to the jungle, staying in caves, searching for Him in so many different places. I met creatures called jinns and fairies who were attracted to me in numbers as I roamed about with them. Fairies can fly to a certain extent, but they cannot go beyond a specific limit, and I did not find God with them. I did learn some of their tricks, but when I realized none of this was God I left them to keep searching.

I went through indescribable difficulties, countless troubles and great danger until I came to the point where it was imperative to understand who my Father was. At that moment I heard a sound, "My son, approach. No one who has ever roamed around searching for Me has ever found Me. I exist everywhere, I am in everything, there is no reason to wander around in search of Me since I exist everywhere. Come, look here, do you see all the messengers, My vice-regents and prophets who left the world, look they are here," and when I looked I saw the prophets seated in groups, may the peace and blessings of God be with them all, each with families and followers gathered around them. There were groups and groups of them, all praying to God. When I looked at their state and heard their sound praising God, when I saw their state of light, it seemed incredibly beautiful, it was wonderful. How can I begin to describe it to you? In that place there were all kinds of flowers and fruit, there were amazing perfumes so beautiful to smell, and many different things you could never imagine, like the beings flying around above these prophets and their followers. When I saw all this the sound came again, "Do you understand?" The Voice called me by name and said, "Do you understand?"

I replied, "I understand a little."

The Voice asked, "Do you recognize these prophets?" and I did recognize them because I had seen them before. I saw that one was a messenger of God I had seen before, another was a vice-regent. When the Voice asked if I recognized them I could say yes to each of the prophets pointed out to me. Then the Voice said, "Look again," and I saw another space above that space where there was another prophet, and another space above that one, and then I could see all seven heavens with the prophets and their disciples in those heavens. When I went beyond the fourth heaven I could see seven heavens more above it and all those who were gathered there, eleven heavens altogether, seven heavens below and eleven above making eighteen, the eighteen thousand universes.

I exclaimed, "O God, I understand this, but I have not seen You. I have heard Your Voice, but I have not seen You. I know this, but I want to see You."

The Voice replied, "You can see Me if you see them. Look at the prophets and you will see Me." Then a range of understanding was given to me: certain sounds spread from that Voice, each sound carrying with it a particular fragrance, a particular light, fragrances and light which struck me. As each blow fell it gave me life and strength, it raised me higher and higher. As each fragrance and each light touched me it lifted me up, it strengthened me. But how can I describe something you cannot even imagine? While I was being raised higher and higher, I looked at each sound, seeing into all the atoms and non-atoms of the eighteen thousand universes. My whole body was resplendent with light, and I could see everything, everything in existence.

Then it was all pointed out to me, "There is *awwal,* the beginning, the time of creation, there is *dunyā,* the world, and over there is *ākhirah,* the realm of God. See the world of the soul, the world of hell and the world of heaven. This is the world of souls, this is the world of hell and this is the world of grace where God and His plenitude exist." The three worlds and their meaning were revealed to me, and I understood them.

I spoke, "This is what You have created, but I want to see You. I want to see my Father." I looked again and wherever I turned I saw a blinding light, everywhere I turned I heard His sound and His speech.

"This is Myself, My son. Wherever you look you will hear My voice, wherever you turn you will hear My sound. This is My form, there is no other form. Nothing is greater than I; everything I created can be contained in a particle within a particle. How could that contain Me? I am so large, so extensive, that I cannot be contained by form. The world is just a particle within a particle, how could you contain Me in that? This is the reason I am called *Allāhu. Hū* is resonance, it is sound and that sound is Myself; light and the sound of that *hū* are Myself." So many explanations were given to me then.

Many more things were revealed after that, and as I was speaking to some of the prophets the sound came again, "Look, look over here, this is what is called prayer." I looked and saw that the earth contained gold; I saw the nine kinds of precious gems shimmering and sparkling, spread through many different places in the earth. The Voice asked, "Do you understand this?"

I said, "Āndavan, O God, this is Your *rahmat,* Your grace, all this is the wealth You created."

The answer came, "No, these are merely the glitters of illusion. It is true they are jewels, it is true they shine, but you cannot compare them to Me. My value is inestimable. These things are valuable in the world and I have given them the name jewels. Whoever finds them thinks they are valuable, but they are only the sparkling gems of illusion. Nevertheless, there is a sparkle within you which is wisdom. Whoever wants to see Me must make that wisdom radiate, make it shine like those precious gems. That is valuable. You can only see Me if you have wisdom, and only if that wisdom shines like light. This radiance must be lit up in the heart, this is the light which can see Me, this is valuable. Now do you understand?"

And I replied, "I do understand."

Then the Voice continued, "Look over here, look at something else," and I saw that all the gems were being covered over with earth. More and more earth covered them, then little shining pebbles started rising up to the surface of the earth, little white pebbles, like the quartz you use in building construction.

There were so many of these pebbles all making a lot of noise shouting, "We are jewels, we are jewels, come see us!" and many, many people started collecting them, taking them home to put in a safe place. The jewels were actually deep in the earth while the quartz which shone like glass on the surface was sought by everyone. Everyone was buying quartz.

"Did you see that, do you understand what it means? Do you know what these precious gems are?" asked the Voice. "They are the future. It means that in the future truth, wisdom, goodness, you and I will be buried, hidden in the earth, just as real gems are hidden deep in the earth. Truth, *gnānam,* divine wisdom and light will be hidden deep within, covered up, while worthless things, the glitters of illusion and satan will be on the surface like those shining pebbles. The people of the world will value these pebbles, they will say they are precious. They will wear them and praise them, like quartz, but the truth which is the real jewel will be hidden. They will keep these worthless things as dear to them at the time of destruction, the time when the world is destroyed.

"In the future truth will be hidden, wisdom will be hidden, the learned will be considered fools and decent people will be thought of as criminals. Criminals will be said to be good and good people will be called dishonest, the learned will be called fools, the virtuous will be called prostitutes, prostitutes will be described as virtuous, what is bad will be called good and what is good will be called bad. Everything will change, people will wear sinful clothing and they will not yearn for God, the truth or heaven. They will bury them and search for the things of hell, for visions of the mind, of the body and the glitters of the world. This is what will happen, so take care," warned the Voice.

"Now look over there, beyond this," and I saw a certain place of worship. Many people were going in dressed in gaudy clothing with bright makeup. On their faces they had new and different kinds of powder, different kinds of makeup. Dressed this way they went to worship God, but inside the building they were not worshiping Him, they were writing love letters to each other, passing the letters around the church, looking everywhere in all directions, taking out their mirrors to put on more lipstick, more makeup, bringing out boxes of powder to dab on their faces. No one followed those who were reciting the prayers and singing, no one was interested in the hymns. There were crowds of people standing outside that building as well, and beyond them were more crowds. The person leading the prayers made wild, excessive movements, jumping up and down, making terrible faces beyond description.

The Voice said, "Look, this is the future. This is not prayer. Remember the prayers you saw before and see how they pray now. You can see the difference. Do you see how they are praying to Me? These are the prayers of illusion, they are not true prayers. This is the way satan prays, do you see? This is what will happen. In the future these glitters will call out saying they are jewels. During the period before the end of the world satan's people, magic, the earth, rocks, beasts, ghosts and illusion will all claim to be gods. They will push themselves to the front insisting, 'I am god, there is no other god but me.' Torpor, intoxicants, magic, fire and earth will boast they are gods, visions of the body and the mind will claim they are gods. You must understand this is going to happen. The people of the world will have certain forces to destroy the truth, to destroy devotion and faith, to destroy the qualities of God and heaven. They will change everything, they will change true prayer saying there is no God, they will manifest injustice and doubt the existence of God. They will prefer the prayers of satan, of hell. They will chant mantras, declaring their importance. You must escape from this."

Then I cried out, "O God please protect me. How long will this last?" and the period of time was disclosed to me. This was sixty years ago, and since that time I can see these changes taking place, I have observed these changes occurring in the last sixty years.

Then the Voice said, "Look over there." I saw millions and millions of idols and gods placed in dark caves, surrounded by countless numbers of disciples. The caves were so dark they had to put an endless number of candles and oil lamps there for the people to find their way in to see their gods. There were five or six hundred priests in charge of cleaning the statues and maintaining them in numerous caves, each pitch dark and filled with millions of different gods which were frightful, ghastly in appearance. None of them looked human, they looked like monkeys with a monkey's teeth, their faces were the faces of lions, tigers, bulls, foxes, wolves and dogs. Some had beaks like a bird or faces like a horse. They all had the teeth and faces of animals. It is impossible to describe these gods, yet people were circling around them, making offerings to them: some slaughtered goats or bulls and offered them to the gods, feeding them their blood; some put brandy, beer and other alcoholic drinks in front of them; some people who were actually being sacrificed to these gods cried out for help, yelling and shrieking; some people circled around them, offering all their wealth and property. These gods had black faces which looked like vampires with teeth for sucking blood. They would reach out to snatch a man, suck his blood and devour him alive.

The Voice said, "Do you see? These are the gods who will rule the world in the future. Look at them, they will all be destroyed by My gaze. They belong to satan's tribe who will capture the world claiming they are god, and they will change everything. This is going to happen in the future." When I looked at each idol it was terrifying. Every offered being was cut and sacrificed in a ghastly manner, the blood sucked from them. I was unable to look at this terrible spectacle any longer, then the Voice said, "Look over there," and I saw four people walking along, shouting out loud about anything that came to their mouth. "Go speak to them," the Voice commanded.

Now the four had fallen into a well, they were all scrambling onto each other's shoulders yelling, "Pick me up, lift me up, get me out of here!" I was told to look into the well and watch them awhile. I could see each of them reaching out for another, grabbing him, trying to throw him up and out of the well.

Suddenly the Voice said, "Look!" and I saw a woman approach who had a certain magic *shakthi,* a force of illusion.

She came right up to the well and asked, "What's the problem, how did you fall into this well?"

"We fell into the well to learn how to climb out of a well," they said to her, to maya or illusion, who had taken the form of a woman.

"All right, get out of there," she said, lifting them from the well and giving them a little food. They ate, found another well and fell in. They did this because they thought if they learned how to climb out they would be able to save anyone else who fell in. This second well was muddy, and once again the woman had to save them. Next they went to an orchard where she told them to water the trees. When they agreed to do this she gave each of them a pot—there is a point I am trying to make here—then they went over to a pond, starting to fight and argue.

The first one said, "This really is a large orchard, how many times do you suppose we will have to fill our pots to water the whole thing?"

Then I came along and asked him, "What are your names?"

"Our names are Know-it-all Fool, Unwitting Fool, Plain Fool and Blind Fool," he replied. These were the names of the four fools.

Now Know-it-all Fool asked the others again, "What should we do? I'll have to think about this, but in order to think, I need a throne to sit on. If I'm going to give you advice I must be seated at a higher elevation than you."

"All right, what you say is true," they agreed, and Unwitting Fool ran to the edge of the pond, bringing back a stone about the size of a marble.

He said, "Right, sit on this throne and preach to us."

"You idiot, how can I sit on that?" he asked.

Then Plain Fool brought back a tiny seashell and said, "Very well, sit on this and preach to us."

"The three of you are amazing idiots," said Know-it-all Fool. "Arrange all the pots one on top of the other, and I will sit on them." They were all earthenware pots, and they put them one on top of the other. Then he climbed to the top and sat down. Naturally, as soon as he sat on them they all broke and crashed down. He fell into them, trapped inside, the last pot hanging around his neck. He yelled, "My brothers, break this pot and pull me out," and so one of the fools ran to the pond to find a big stick. The word for pot in Tamil can also mean skull, and when Know-it-all Fool told them to break the pot around his neck they thought he was telling them to break his skull. They smashed his head with the stick until he fell unconscious among the broken pots.

Plain Fool said, "Hey, give me that stick," as he snatched it away from Unwitting Fool, "You have only freed his legs. Look, just his legs are sticking out, watch me, I will free his whole body," and he landed a sharp blow smack in the middle of Know-it-all Fool's rear end.

All the pots broke even more now, but the blow was so hard that Know-it-all Fool fell almost unconscious again as he started moaning, "Water, get me some water."

When he heard this Unwitting Fool ran to get some water in his hands, although by the time he came back there was nothing left. Plain Fool said, "How can you bring enough in your hands?" and he ran to bring water on a small leaf.

Then Blind Fool said, "How can you bring him out of his faint with that much water?" and he ran back to get some in a tiny seashell. You see, these events will actually take place in the future.

Next they decided the only way to revive Know-it-all Fool was to put him into the pond itself, and they carried him over to drop him into the pond. In his struggle to escape he swallowed water, was gasping for breath and drowning until he managed to blurt, "Get me out of here," as the waves pushed him back to the banks of the pond.

Since all four of them had lost their pots, they were worried the woman might be angry with them if they did not water the trees in the orchard. They thought, "We will carry the pond to the garden, that is the only thing to do. We'll lift it out and bring it to the orchard then it will be easy for us and the dear lady will praise us." They broke off some thin, spiny branches of the *murunga*, the drumstick tree, made four sticks with them, and then tried to pick up the pond on the end of these four sticks. As they pressed down on the sticks it made them bend. This made them think they were lifting the pond.

Someone who was passing by along the road asked, "What are you trying to do?"

They answered, "We're trying to carry the pond to the orchard, so it will be easy to water."

"How can you carry a pond?" asked the passerby, "If you can carry this pond you can carry the whole world, how can you do that?"

"Idiot, how dare you try to advise us! You obviously don't understand our brilliant ideas. This is our kingdom which means you can't understand what we're trying to do. We rule here; if imbeciles like you try to advise us we'll beat you up." They picked up their sticks to hit the passerby, yelling, "People like you must be destroyed because you are trying to ruin our ideas. Don't ever try to advise us again, we're going to carry this pond to the orchard." Then they showed the passerby how their sticks moved, "Look, see how the pond is moving." The passerby tried to explain to them it was only the sticks moving, not the pond, but they kept hitting him until he ran away.

Then the Voice said to me, "Now do you understand? In the future, people like these four fools will govern the world, people who are wise will be unable to rule at that time because they will be chased away. Ignorant people like the fools who throw people into a well to practice rescuing them will rule the world. People like them will try to carry a pond to an orchard. This will be their kind of wisdom. Those who are virtuous or devoted, those who have beautiful qualities and pray to God will have no place in this world as it comes to an end. This world will become satan's kingdom where everything is made into a god. They will see to it that God is forgotten and that fools like Know-it-all Fool, Unwitting Fool, Plain Fool and Blind Fool rule the world. Understand that this is the time when the world will end, when people will not believe in God."

Many, many such things were revealed to me. What is the significance of the orchard? The orchard is a garden which represents the heart, a garden of fruit, a garden of flowers; there are many kinds of fruit to taste and many flowers to smell in this garden of our heart. The woman told them to take truth from the pond of grace and wisdom, she told them to pour it on the fruit and eat, but they could only destroy the truth. They tried to carry the pond itself which represents the world, falsehood. Instead of bringing the water of wisdom to the garden, they brought ignorance, falsehood, lies, intoxicants, torpor and birth.

The Voice said, "In the future, you must try to escape from the world which will belong to them. All My children must try to escape from them. If you stay with them they will murder you or chase you away, they will destroy you or make you disappear. Escape from these people," the Voice commanded. Everything was revealed to me, everything was explained to me as I went beyond, farther and farther, to see my Father. I had so many experiences. At the end of the world magic, mantras, tantras, different forms of worship and prayer, idols and satan will manifest. This is the word of God which was revealed to me. It will happen. Only a very little truth will remain, just like the time when the gems were buried deep in the earth and cheap glass stones became precious. Swamis, gurus, religious leaders and many gods will be the false glitters, the surface stones, stones you use to make a road. They will be nothing more than gravel on the surface of a road while the precious jewels stay buried deep below the earth.

Falsehood, ignorance, false wisdom, darkness, torpor, satan, and maya or illusion will all rise to the surface. They are even accepted now in the world today, and this is a sign of the forthcoming destruction. This is the reason the seasons are changing, the reason why floods and such destructive storms have appeared. Because the truth of God, the wonders of God and the prayers of God are disappearing, the seasons have been changing. In the past it was not like this in America. Now there are terrible floods, certain destructive winds and new, appalling diseases have appeared. Little children die of dreadful diseases, older people are developing new kinds of cancer and about seventy-five percent of the population have poor eyesight.

Unjust people have become the leaders of nations, evil people are praised, truth is hidden, the corrupt are praised while good people are humiliated. This is destruction, the time of destruction when what is good is insulted and evil is exalted. All this was shown to me by my Father when I was young, clear signs which I see now. Young children no longer listen to their parents, they do whatever their minds tell them to do. They use marijuana, cocaine and alcohol which make evil qualities manifest—their good thoughts disappear and they manifest evil. The four virtuous qualities, modesty, reserve, sincerity and fear of wrongdoing, are disappearing. This is the way destruction approaches. When I look around I see this happening everywhere, in London, America, Ceylon and many other places as well.

Everything has become artificial, everything seems copied. Studies and learning are not original, prayer is not original, conduct is not original, clothing is not original or natural, even nature is becoming artificial. The things we do are changing from their original, natural state to an unnatural state. Our prayers are becoming unnatural. There is no pure wisdom, everything is artificial, unnatural and copied; all this signifies the end. The seven levels of consciousness or wisdom are disappearing now, levels with which human beings can come to understand by using the wisdom they already have. Ghosts, demons, famine, disease, poverty, problems, wars, quarrels, thefts, falsehood, murder and destruction prevail now.

My children, you must search for your Father with truth. He has no form. He exists as the heart within the heart. He is the gracious One, the marvelous, luminous One who exists as wisdom within wisdom. We must find true prayer, we need wisdom, we need the qualities of God. We must search for them because the time of destruction is very close and we must escape. Understand that if you search for the truth you will have trouble and many problems, yet your Father will always protect you. Do not worry about the difficulties, just search for your Father during your lifetime. For this you need *īmān,* you need the faith, certitude and determination that whatever suffering you undergo, your Father will save you. No matter what suffering you may know, you must never waver in certitude or faith. Your wisdom must never change.

God is formless, He is the One who exists wherever you look, He is
with you day and night. He is here every moment; you must have the eye
which can see Him and the faith to search for Him. Wisdom is the eye.
You need certitude and determination to search for Him. His qualities
are the grace with which you can see Him. Do not let go just because of
pain or sadness or sorrow. God's truth is like a shore for all suffering. The
waves of the ocean try to break past that shore, but they cannot. Waves
cannot be still, they come with the intention of breaking up the shore to
destroy the world, yet they can only strike the shore and return to the
ocean. In this way, truth is like a shore, grace is a shore, truth, wisdom
and the qualities of God are a shore for the ocean of maya. The waves of
maya will slam against them, but they can only return to maya. Disease,
poverty and troubles will strike you, however if you have the truth, they
cannot penetrate, they will recede. They come to break you, they will hit
you, but they cannot destroy you. The profits and losses of the world will
try to destroy you, yet if your faith, your certitude and wisdom are strong
they do recede. They will keep coming time after time, but if your faith is
strong and you take no notice of them, nothing can happen to you.

You must have our Father's grace, His wisdom, His patience. You must
acquire His plenitude, not the glitters of maya, the magic, the mantras,
the forms and words like the *om* and *am* and *sam* or *jam* of yoga, words
which are merely like the jam you eat. The world puts everything into
this jam promising you it is sweet, yet it is really bitter or salty or sour,
and once you eat it you have to eliminate it. This is only a bathroom thing;
do not acquire it. If you eat that jam believing it to be sweet, you will end
up having to eliminate it in the bathroom. Do not acquire the habit. God,
our Father, is very tasty. His light is plentiful and you must try to acquire
this truth.

My children, there are so many things that happened to me during
my life. I am only telling you one very small point I remember. I have
given you just a little description of what really happened, these lessons of
mine, what I experienced, what I went through. When I searched for my
Father I found that treasure, and this is the reason why the things you
offer me are unacceptable. I cannot accept your studies. If you bring me a
god I cannot accept it, if you bring me magic I cannot accept it, if you
bring me a guru I cannot accept it. Why not? Because I have had all this
experience, I have had the experience of this kind of magic, this kind of
study, I have seen the gurus, learned the mantras and thrown them away.
What I offer may be hard for you to accept, nevertheless if you acquire

wisdom, you will accept it. If you have had these experiences and know the truth from this experience, how can you accept anything but that truth? With your idea of truth from the experiences you have had, you might not accept my truth. It might be hard for even a few of you to accept it, yet if you have wisdom, if you truly understand, you will accept it.

The things you want can be bought in a store; it is easy to buy things from a store or the supermarket, but the treasure you need to purchase from your Father is very hard to acquire. If you go to the supermarket you pick out something and pay for it. In this world you can buy a mantra for fifty or a hundred dollars. For an additional hundred and twenty-five dollars they might even say they will show you the light. That's easy, they are supermarket products, but the real Light, what you must buy from your Father Himself is hard to find. To do that you need to search for wisdom, you need to acquire the qualities of God. You need to understand and reflect on this with wisdom. Now the seasons are changing and destruction is coming closer. In the little time you have left you must try to escape, try to reach our Father and merge with Him. A few children must try because if they succeed they might be able to prevent this destruction, this famine and great danger. There are a few children who might be able to prevent this.

May God grant you the wisdom to travel the path of truth. Now that satan's rule is almost established, since his rule predominates today, you have to be very careful, you have to think each thought deliberately, using wisdom. Always have faith, certitude and determination because this is the power of God. Everything you see on the outside is illusion, merely small powers, but God is the real power within us. To understand this power you need wisdom and the qualities of God; with these two you can understand His power. My children, jewels of my eyes, please think hard, try to walk the right path. It is my duty to reveal my own experience to you, and it is with your own experience that you must search for your Father. That is a good thing to do.

This is the way things are. I had this experience I have described, and there is so much more that I have seen and heard. All the glitters of the world are supermarket things that will end in the bathroom, they will become the kingdom of hell. Please therefore, reflect on what I have told you, reflect with wisdom because that will be a very good thing to do. *Āmīn.*

July 15, 1975

2 | The Path of Duty

INTERVIEWER: Could Bawa tell us something about his life?

BAWA MUHAIYADDEEN: My brother, most of my life is over now, and I do not usually concern myself with the story of my life, a life devoted to the love of my children. Living that way, I have had to face many difficulties in the world. It is quite hard to direct my children along a good, true path with good, true wisdom, and since I am dedicated to guiding them, involving myself entirely in their lives and their progress, I do not notice what happens to me.

Duty seems to be my only purpose. I do not look for comfort in life, I do not look for happiness, I do not try to create my own history. I care only that the qualities of my children be the qualities of God and the prophets who came before us. My purpose is to teach my children the way of the prophets who advised us in the past. My dedication is to bring my children's qualities to the exalted level the prophets have described. This is my history, this has become my history.

I came to Philadelphia for the first time in 1971 when I was invited here by my child Bob Demby, who is now one of the presidents of this Fellowship, and a few others. At that time we lived in a house on 46th Street, then I returned to Sri Lanka a year later. When I came back on my second visit I stayed, first at the same house, then later in 1973 we moved to this Fellowship House, and now it is 1979. I stay awhile, coming and going back to Sri Lanka until the children here cry and write so many letters begging me to return, I come back to comfort them. This is what I have been doing in the United States.

I do not say much about myself or my history. Even in Ceylon, in Sri Lanka, my whole purpose is to direct my children to a good, true path. I go to the farm in Puliyankulam because we have to work the farm to feed our children there. Sometimes children come from far away who are ill, and we have to look after them, other people come possessed by ghosts and demons to be cured, others come who are destitute, penniless, and we help them. I work on the farm day and night to give the proceeds to the poor. Any money after expenses I give to the poor. Attending to the needs of the children, doing my duty to them, serving God by urging them to walk on God's path has been my duty, and I do this kind of work in both Sri Lanka and America. Three-quarters of the American children here have been to Sri Lanka with me, they have seen the amount of work I do there. I do not really like to talk about myself, I would rather spend time doing my duty instead of talking about myself. If you ask me to talk about myself I will tell you what I have experienced, and if I mention those experiences, you will find most of it is suffering, most of it is pain. What I see in this world looks like pain and suffering to me.

There is only one place where there is peace, a place inside the *qalb,* the inner heart, where *Allāhu ta'ālā Nāyan,* our exalted Lord who is God, lives with the *Rasūl,* the Prophet Muhammad ☪. They live together there in the same place where all the prophets live who came as witnesses to the existence of God, the mighty One. This is the place, the only place where you can find peace and comfort. Anywhere else you look in the world seems to be just pain and suffering. If you are dedicated to performing your duty in the world you have to do it without attachment, without partiality or favor, you must do it without selfishness or thought of profit. You have to love all living things and treat them as your own life, recognizing the hunger of others as your own, recognizing the happiness of others as your own, the peace of others as your own, the joy of others as your own.

When a man does his duty this way, all he sees in life is difficulty and hardship. A man in this state must burn himself down to give light to others. He must be like the wax in a candle, burning himself down to give light to others. That is his duty. In this state, what comfort is there for the candle to enjoy, what happiness does the candle enjoy? What can we say? This is the state of a person who wants to do his duty to God, he has to burn himself down to give light to the others in the world, and that is my life.

INTERVIEWER: Why did you choose to have the Fellowship's location in Philadelphia? Is there any significance in this?

BAWA MUHAIYADDEEN: The lady from California seated behind you came to see me in Sri Lanka back in 1960. She came to see me almost twenty years ago, staying with me in Jaffna for six months. Even at that time I was doing the same duties at the Fellowship there in the ashram, and what I did was exactly what I described before. I would take her with me when I went into the jungle to gather healing herbs for the people who were sick, and we worked on the farm. At the end of six months I said to her, "It is time for you to go back to America, I might come to America later on. You go back, attend to your duties and it is possible, if Allah wills, that I will come to America in the future." I told her this in 1960, but in 1950 I wrote a book in which I mention I will be going to America. This book has a story about a tree planted in an arid desert, a story where I mention I will be going to the west. That was in 1950, and accordingly, in 1971 four or five of my children invited me with love and urgency to come to America.

Before I arrived at 46th Street in Philadelphia for my first visit, Bob Demby, Carolyn Secretary, Zoharah Simmons and some others sitting here arranged for me to come.

They formed a society for that purpose, to invite me here. I did not come to Philadelphia with the idea of establishing a fellowship. There is only one Fellowship and that is Allah's. There is only one family and only one Fellowship. The whole world is one Fellowship. We are all the children of Adam ☺, and Allah is in charge of that Fellowship. I did not come here to establish a fellowship, I came here to see my brothers and sisters, to see my children, this is the reason why I came.

When I arrived they called the house I lived in a fellowship; the fellowship is a house, this is what they call a fellowship. When you give birth to a child you give the child a name, do you not? In the same way, these children found a name for this house. There are many kinds of names. There are the ninety-nine names of Allah which are His qualities and actions, His virtuous conduct, His love, His duties, they are the ninety-nine *wilāyats* or powers of Allah. Then there are the three thousand gracious attributes and His countless, limitless sounds of grace to which you give names. You give names to everyone who is born, do you not? In the same way, these children gave this house a name they liked. They described it as Sufi and gave it a name. Sufi has a profound meaning, Fellowship also has a deep meaning. But the name they gave is not different from anything else. They merely gave it a name just as you name a child when it is born. There are sixteen or seventeen branches which also use the name fellowship. But the whole world is just one Fellowship, and there is only One who is in charge, Allah alone. So what can you say about the significance of a name?

He is the One in charge, He is the One responsible for all three worlds, for *awwal, dunyā* and *ākhirah,* the time of creation, this world and the realm of God. Allah is in charge of these three, the universe of the *rūh* where the souls began, the *dunyā* which is this created world, and *ākhirah,* where we return to Him. Allah is the ruler of these three Fellowships. They have merely given this place a name. They call it a fellowship, but the only One ultimately responsible for it is Allah.

INTERVIEWER: What happens to this Fellowship when you are no longer here to lead your children?

BAWA MUHAIYADDEEN: Allah will be here, will He not? This is not my responsibility, is it? That entire *sukūn,* the tiny diacritical mark which is the world, is supported by the *alif,* the letter which is One, Allah. He is here no matter what happens. There is no reason for us to carry this burden which is His office and His responsibility. We say *al-hamdu lillāh,* all praise belongs to You, *tawakkul-'alallāh,* whatever happens is Your will. It is not my work to be concerned with what will happen.

My brother, there are ninety-nine *wilāyats* of Allah which are the powers He uses to administer His rule. If you take one tiny particle of any one of His ninety-nine qualities, cut it into a hundred million pieces, then pick one of these pieces to examine, you will see ninety-nine particles inside revolving around each other without touching, ninety-nine particles revolve without touching each other. Then if you take one of those hundred million particles, divide that particle into fifty million pieces and take one of these particles to examine with a microscope, again you will see ninety-nine particles revolving around each other without touching. If you take that particle, divide it into five million pieces and take one of these particles, you will see ninety-nine particles again revolving around each other without touching. If you take one of those particles, divide it into five hundred thousand pieces, you see the ninety-nine revolving around each other without touching. If you take one of those particles, divide it into fifty thousand pieces and pick any one of these particles, again you see the ninety-nine revolving around each other without touching. Then if you take one of those particles, cut it into six thousand, six hundred and sixty-six pieces and take one of these particles to examine, you see the ninety-nine revolving around one another without touching. If you take one of those particles, cut it into three hundred and thirteen pieces and select any one of these particles, again you will see the ninety-nine revolving around each other without touching. If you take one of those pieces, cut it into ninety-nine particles and take one of these particles, again you see ninety-nine revolving around each other without touching.

Then if you take one *alif,* one Arabic letter (I), the 'a,' and cut it open, you will see the ninety-nine particles inside revolving one around the other without touching. If you take one sound from this, cut it open, and if you keep cutting and examining, you find the power increasing, more sound, more power, more light. And if you keep cutting, go farther in, that light will pull you in, that power will draw you in and that which is you will die. Beyond this you are dead, you no longer exist. Your wisdom dies, everything dies, you are drawn into it and that power alone remains. This is His responsibility, He alone exists there. And since this is so my brother, what do you have to do in this world? Only your duty. Whatever will happen tomorrow is *tawakkul-'alallāh,* you surrender the responsibility to Him; whatever happens now, you say *al-hamdu lillāh,* all praise belongs to You, O God.

INTERVIEWER: *As-salāmu 'alaikum,* may the peace of God be with you.

BAWA MUHAIYADDEEN: *Wa 'alaikumus-salām,* and may the peace of God also be with you. Let us unload our burdens and give them to Allah. Put them on His ship. He is responsible for everything. Unload your burdens and leave them in His care for perfect peace. This will give you peace.

October 5, 1979

3 | THE TREE THAT FELL TO THE WEST

L et me tell you a story about the man who wanted to plant a tree in the desert. Once there was a wise man living in the desert who noticed there was no water, there were no trees, no shade and no place for travelers and animals to sit and rest. He thought to himself, "I will plant at least one tree to offer shade to those who come by."

And so he planted a seed, but everyone who came past ridiculed and mocked him, "Who is this idiot, this madman trying to plant a tree in the desert? How will a tree ever grow here? There is no water here, and not only that, there are sandstorms, there is lightning and thunder. He must be really crazy!"

But the wise man kept watering the young plant with the water he brought from far away, guarding it carefully. Soon roots began to grow, then branches. It grew higher and higher until it could draw up its own food and water through the roots. Soon animals and wayfarers came to sit under the tree because it was the only place there was to rest, but they left it dirty with their excrement and garbage. Even so, the wise man just kept cleaning it up, continuing to take care of the tree.

The tree grew from the depths of the earth to the highest heaven, bearing excellent, endless fruit which satisfied the hunger, thirst and fatigue of those who came. Its branches and leaves gave shade and rest to those who were tired, but once the tree was discovered, people started fighting about it, claiming it as their tree and their fruit. So the wise man who had cared for the tree left saying, "You can have the profits of this tree."

Birds like parrots and mynahs would come to eat the fruit high up on the tree, then people put up nets to trap them, to stop them from eating even though these people could only reach the fruit on the lower branches. The very same people who had ridiculed the wise man for planting the tree now claimed it was theirs. Their envy had made them ridicule him, and their envy and jealousy made them claim the tree as their own. They fought and fought to such an extent they wanted to cut it down so that other people would not benefit from it.

That tree was such an amazing tree, growing all the way from *awwal* to *ākhirah,* from the time of creation to the realm of God. There was so much fruit, that jinns and fairies, birds and human beings could all eat from this tree. Whoever came could take some and be satisfied. Even the fruit that fell off the tree was eaten by animals, insects and worms in the earth.

Eventually they cut the tree down. Because the tree had reached up to the heavens, it fell from the east to the west, and now the fruit and the flowers were a benefit in the west. The trunk remained in the east, but the taste, the fruit and flowers fell in the west where the people were able to profit from its amazing flavors.

The things I wrote about in *Guru Mani* back in 1942 all happened; what is left in the east are the trunk and roots of the tree. Some people have collected these parts of the tree and preserved them, but the fruit, the benefit fell in the west. When God does something He knows what happens in the present, what happens in the future, what happened in the past and what is happening at this very instant. This is all in the book, it is history now.

Whatever you do for God who is our Creator is known to Him before you do it. Before you do something He has already said you would do this. At the present He tells you what will happen in the future, at the end He tells you what happened at the beginning. He reveals certain secrets ahead of time about birth, death and what is happening now. He warns you about what will come in the future. He knows the duty you will do and the reward you will receive for it. He tells you this ahead of time, and you have to do it to fulfill His word. You must understand this. There is a deep meaning here.

Even though there may be only a small group of children now in the west, God has given you the taste of this fruit, the ripe fruit of *gnānam,* that divine wisdom from the kingdom of God, because the tree fell here. The kingdom of God belongs to you. Be very careful not to let it go. Preserve it, do your duty and know the taste. This is not just a game, this is not magic and not a mantra, this is something you should not neglect. Try to savor the taste with your wisdom, do this duty. This is the right thing to do, children, please do it.

May 24, 1975 and *February 20, 1976*

4 | Bawa Muhaiyaddeen ⓢ As A Young Boy

When I was young I misbehaved a lot, I was small for my age and quite naughty. When I was six or seven the disciples, who had long beards and were fifty or sixty years of age, used to sit in a row with the sheikh before them, and I always tried to sit right between two of them. The sheikh would close his eyes to meditate, recite or study, but I knew nothing about the things they were studying. And so I would look around carefully, then quickly, quietly pinch one of the disciples two or three times, really hard! The first one would look around and wipe his eyes, then I would pinch the other one. My only occupation was to pinch and wait to see what happened next. If a disciple started reciting certain verses with great concentration, I would creep up to him and bite his ear, then sit back down, very quiet, until I crept up to bite someone else's ear.

Some of the disciples would actually cry in pain. If the sheikh opened his eyes and found them crying he would ask, "What happened, why are you crying?" but not one of them would open his mouth to say anything, and I would look down, my head bent as though I were meditating deeply. The next day I would sit between two others and do the same thing. I did this repeatedly; when I finished one round I would start all over on the first group of disciples. Once the sheikh saw me biting someone's ear and said, "You'd better sit beside me." I sat at his side and when he was quiet, I was very quiet. Because his disciples were facing me I made grotesque faces, grinning at them, trying to make them laugh. I did things like that.

Occasionally the sheikh took us for a walk, then I would make a run at the disciples, butting them with my head from behind, and of course they would fall. I did many naughty things like that which were quite natural at this stage. Even though I did all these bad things, when the sheikh asked me a question I could give an appropriate answer, better than all the other disciples although I did not study. This was God's grace—I did not study but I could answer his questions. The other disciples could not answer his questions, but whenever he asked me something I was able to give a suitable answer.

Yet when the sheikh gave me a book to read, I could not read it. He loved me so much, and he would say lovingly, "Please read this." I knew the book by heart and I would recite it from memory. The sheikh understood this was unique; he also understood I had no fear and he respected me for this.

Many people came to see the sheikh, people with diseases or childless people who wanted children. Once a woman came crying, falling at the feet of the sheikh, "O *nāyan,* O great lord, I want children, yet I have no children and it is so painful for me."

The sheikh replied, "You must live as your destiny determines, and there are no children in your destiny." The sheikh knew everything; he told her she had to live as her destiny ruled, he also told her that what he said was correct because he knew everyone's *nasīb,* everyone's destiny. The woman brought offerings of gold, pleading with him for a child, but the sheikh said, "There are no children in your destiny because if you have a child, you will die."

The woman wept and cried, pouring sand on her head, cursing her destiny, "O my sheikh, you have given me a death sentence."

The sheikh repeated, "You will live for only eight months of your pregnancy if you have a child, you will die in your ninth month. Asking for a child is asking for death." The woman kept beating her head, crying and cursing her destiny, and I watched all this.

Even though I was naughty I did have great compassion for people, and so I said to her, "Please don't cry, you will have a boy and live a long time, you can go now." The sheikh became very angry when he heard me say this. I repeated my words, "You will give birth to a boy and live a long time, don't worry, you can go. You will live forty or fifty years." I said the words that came to my mouth.

Later the woman conceived a child, and as she was ready to give birth her husband came to tell the sheikh, who pronounced, "What I said was her destiny can never be changed. The words I uttered cannot be changed because it is God's destiny. Since she has conceived she will die in her ninth month. What I say will happen." Then the woman died with the child still inside her body.

As the sheikh and I were walking along we saw a funeral procession. When I asked him, "What's happening over there? I have never seen anything like this before."

The sheikh replied, "What is happening is what I said would happen."
I did not understand and asked again, "What *is* happening?"

"*Janāzah,* a funeral, this is the lady who asked for the favor of a child."

"Is that who it is? Then let her get up," I said, "Let her get up, let her
sit straight up." Her body started to move. "Let Allah raise her up, let her
sit up." They had to put the funeral bier down as her body started moving.
The sheikh, several people and I were all there watching. As soon as the
bier was placed down on the ground the woman got up, looked at me,
and my face must have seemed different because she just shook her head
without recognizing me. They dismantled the bier and threw it into the
grave along with all the other funeral things that cannot be used again.
All the funeral things went to the grave except the woman, she was not
buried.

I can remember she was about twenty-four years old when the child
was born, and they came to the sheikh with offerings of gems on one tray,
gold and fruit on another tray. The sheikh was extremely angry. He pointed
to me and said, "Give this to him."

But I said, "Take it to the sheikh, take it to the sheikh."

The sheikh said, "No, this is for you, you take it."

I told them, "No, it is for the sheikh and for God, it is for you and for
God, not for me. I don't know anything at all."

After that the sheikh tried to hurt me. He tried pushing me down the
mountainside, but when he did his arm was suddenly paralyzed. Although
he was a very great sheikh envy overcame him, and he intended me harm.
Just before he died he spoke, "I did not realize who you are. You are the
Qutbuz-zamān, the *Qutb,* the supremely enlightened being of this era, but
I did not realize it. You will be the sheikh, a mother to all the children." mother

I was very young at the time, only eleven, and answered, "I am only a
boy with no idea how to do that." But he understood this, saying those
words just as he was about to die. They split a rock, buried the sheikh,
and then the people whom I had pinched and whose ears I had bitten
became good. I was eleven years old at the time.

I did many naughty things. After this a king who was childless looked
after me, but all those who looked after me, who loved me and tried to
raise me, all of them passed away. Those who tried to kill me for my wealth
were united in their effort, yet those who raised me in love all passed away.

We all do naughty, obnoxious things. A child who is naughty in his or
her youth will be good later on, a child who is quiet when he is young
will misbehave later on. Very often a child who behaves well early on can

grow up to misbehave. Those who eat too much when they are young lose weight later on, and those who eat just a little when they are young often become fat when they grow up. Even our actions change as we mature, we do less as we grow older.

There was a time when I did not eat, but I eat now, I eat a lot now. I have been eating a lot for ten or eleven years. If a bird eats a single seed it fills its belly, does it not? Is that not food? A bird and a man are similar because they both fill their stomachs. For a bird it takes only a seed. Man also fills his stomach until he is satisfied, like the bird. The real *rizq*, the real food however, is minute, only an atom in size. We give hay to the *nafs*, the base desires, because the *nafs* want bulk, but the actual *rizq* within any food is just an atom from God, and that is what satisfies, what makes even water given as *rizq* enough. When God gives an atom, a particle as nourishment, it is enough. We have to think about each and every life, analyze and study every living thing. Human beings must analyze the actions, qualities and goodness in all living things.

When you split open the truth and analyze it, you discover the secret, and you will finally realize God. When you understand the truth you understand that secret. You have to analyze the truth, split it open, understand it and then analyze whatever you are attached to. Focus your attention on it, analyze it. Attachments are like magnets, the poison in your life that kills you. They destroy God's truth, His qualities and His justice. If you are attached, that attachment will kill you. Destroy whatever it is you are attached to or it will kill your very life. Whatever mind, desire and the world want, all this must be controlled, and whatever wisdom loves must be fed with goodness. This will be good for your life.

December 29, 1981

5 | BAWA MUHAIYADDEEN ﷺ THE KING

QUESTION: Can you describe the path to God?

BAWA MUHAIYADDEEN: That is a good question, a question I once asked long ago during a time in my life when I was wealthy, rich with money and land. Let me tell you a bit of that history.

There was once a king who had been childless for many years, ruling eighteen regions, each approximately the size of Pennsylvania. Because he had no children he pledged himself to God, vowing to perform service to Him for twelve years; in return, he hoped God would reward him with a child. Over those twelve years he built a number of churches, temples and mosques, doing his duty in each of these places of worship.

Among the king's many relatives and friends were three prominent families who served as overseers for certain areas on the land. Since these three families were childless as well, they had also pledged themselves to God's service for twelve years, hoping they would be given children. Finally, the king and the families came to the end of their twelfth year of service to God. Each year this king and these three families took part in a festival at the Murugan temple. It was the king's custom to make his vows at the Bawa shrine which was on a mountain just above the Murugan temple, but below the mosque.

The night before the festival the king had a vision which told him to go to the Bawa shrine where he would find a child on the steps leading up to it. On the day of the festival the king was walking towards the staircase leading to the shrine when his friend, a *chettiyar,* a rich merchant, and his wife were also walking there, a little ahead of the king. The merchant and his wife who were childless had also been praying to God, doing service to Him for twelve years, hoping to have a child. The driver of the cart they had hired to bring everything they needed for the festival walked behind them, carrying a huge sack.

As they climbed they saw a baby lying on the steps, and when they looked more closely they discovered an ugly child, filthy, covered with oozing sores, the flies buzzing around and sitting on them. The smell was terrible; they were disgusted. Even though they had prayed to God for a baby, as soon as they saw this child they walked around it and continued on their way. The driver, however, put down his heavy sack and went over to the baby, noticing that although the baby was filthy and covered with sores, it was wrapped in a white silk blanket. He picked the child up, embracing it to his heart.

The rich merchant looked back, yelled at the driver and told him to put the baby down, to get on with his job. "Why have you picked up this filthy corpse of a baby? Put it down and get back to work!"

But the driver replied softly, "This child is alive; someone, perhaps his mother, abandoned him. How can we just leave him here?"

The merchant ordered, "Either you leave it here or I will get someone else to do your job!"

The driver answered, "Well then, I don't want your job, I'd rather have the baby. Hire anyone you like, I could never leave the baby here like that!" And so the merchant and his wife found another man coming up the path whom they hired to carry their goods, then continued on to the temple.

Meanwhile, the king had started up the steps and noticed the driver with a baby. "Could this be the child meant for me?" he wondered, but continued on to the temple where he met his friend, the merchant, telling him about his vision. The merchant said he had seen a child on the steps leading to the shrine, but it was disgusting, covered with oozing sores. He told the king that the driver had taken the child. Now the king thought to himself, "I saw a man with a baby, and God said there was a baby here for me, it must have been that baby." He retraced his steps looking for the driver.

When he found him and saw the child he was revolted thinking, "This disgusting child was probably not meant for me," but he asked the driver anyway, "Will you give me this child?"

He replied, "This child does not belong to the right class for you."

The king thought briefly and agreed, "Yes, that must be so," then continued on his way up the mountain to make his vows.

The baby was, in fact, really meant for the king, nevertheless the driver took it home to his two other children. The moment they reached his house the sores on the baby disappeared. He became a happy, beautiful child, smiling and gaining weight quickly. Meanwhile the rich merchant was displeased with the new driver and called upon his friend, the king, asking if he could send for the previous driver and put him back in his old job. He did not want to do it himself because he thought the driver might refuse him. The king summoned the driver, and since it was the king, he could not refuse.

The next day the driver came to the palace holding the baby in his arms, and the king saw a beautiful baby, smiling and happy with a clear, pale greenish complexioned skin, light radiating from his face. He smiled at the king who melted at once. "This is indeed the child God meant for me," he thought as he asked the driver, "Will you give me this child? I will give you anything you want for him."

The driver replied, "I will give you my life if you ask, but not this baby. This child was given to me by God, and even if I am made a beggar I cannot give him up."

The king said, "You are right, this child was given by God, and since he was, he can be my child, yours, and God's child too. You must understand that I can certainly look after this baby better than you can, so why not come to live here in my palace? I will give you a job and you will see him every day." The driver thought about it and agreed it would be best for the child. Placing the baby in the king's custody, he came to live at the palace where the king bestowed wealth and land on him, letting him see the infant every day.

I was actually that child. They put me in a solid gold cradle studded with gems and silver. They gave me everything imaginable in the world, and that is why the king's relatives became jealous. They started a rumor that the driver had found a baby in the jungle and put him on the steps along the king's path to extract money from him, then they hatched a plot to kill both the driver and myself, planning how to divide our wealth. While all this was going on the driver suddenly died and everything the king had given him became mine. Now the king's family became even more jealous. They hired assassins to kill me, but when they came up to my cradle I suddenly became invisible; every time they tried to kill me they could not find me.

Three months later the king died, leaving me the whole kingdom and all his wealth, yet as the property and wealth accumulated, the difficulties also multiplied. The rich merchant and his wife cared for me until I was one-and-a-half years old when the merchant and his wife were killed in an accident. Then their fortune also became mine, mountains of gold, gems and silver, more land than can be imagined, and so a Brahman treasurer was appointed as trustee of my holdings. By then I could talk a little, but

I was in great danger. Now God sent me a guru who took me away. He hid me in a cave on top of a mountain where he concealed the key to my treasury beneath the bark of a tree. While I lived in that cave the assassins searched for me in vain; whenever they tried to climb the mountain it would seem to grow higher and higher, they could never reach the top.

Only the guru approached me as I ran around and played every day. Even though the guru was so busy, he always brought my food and fruit himself. This went on until I was five years old and quite naughty. Near the cave there was a pond filled with crocodiles. I would amuse myself by catching them and climbing up on their backs to ride around the pond. I liked that, riding among the lotus flowers, passing the time quite happily.

While I was playing in the pond during my sixth year, one of the assassins finally caught sight of me, ran up, seized me and threw me into the dam. I remember it was at one end of the pond. This killer and two others threw me into a crumbling section at the middle of the dam and started to cover me up with sand, burying me until just a little area of my face remained uncovered. As they were about to close up that last little place, a snake appeared and bit one of them who died on the spot. It slid towards the second assassin, bit him and he fell dead too. When the third one tried to run away he suddenly became blind, and I could hear the guru calling my name as he came running frantically to dig me out. The snake had already disappeared by the time he finished washing me in the pond. I kept asking him to bring the dead men back to life again. But he said it was God's command that they should die, and when I asked him to restore the blind man's sight, he replied again that it was God's command that he should be blind.

Once I was washed clean I ran to the dead men and brought them back to life; then I went to the blind man and gave him his sight back. They groveled at my feet, begging forgiveness. "Why did you do this?" I asked.

"Because of your land," they explained, "That land was meant for us and we want it back."

I said, "That may be true, but whose property is it anyway? The person who owned it until lately is dead now. Well never mind, if you want it you can have it. Bring the trustee to me," and they ran to get him.

I instructed him to transfer the land to them, but he commented, "Until you are twenty-one you have no control over the money or the land."

I argued, "I am of age, I can give my property to anyone I want," but he would not hear of it. Then I said, "Well you can have a share too, if

you like." Of course that silenced him immediately, and I divided the
property giving some to the trustee, some to the assassins, some to others.
Everyone got what they wanted, but I reserved a small piece of land, about
the size of Pennsylvania, for the people who lived there to farm.

At the age of seven I left this place for another mountain, going to
study with another guru. I stayed there for eighteen years, sometimes doing
things other than studying. I liked to tease, pinch and bite the other
students, I liked to do that. I did learn things, but I did mischievous things
too. That was my mischief, biting and pinching, but knowledge was my
destiny and I did receive it. I would fight with the guru, contradict, even
argue with him until he became suspicious of me. What he said was right,
but sometimes I would beat him down, override what he said. He became
so jealous he decided to kill me, instructing his disciples to throw me off
the mountain, and one day they did push me over the edge. I rolled down
over and over for two miles, but I did not die. It seemed a funny kind of
game to me, because all I was aware of as I came hurtling down the
mountain was a hand stretched out to support me. When I got to the
bottom, I climbed back up the mountain to the ashram, arriving there
before the others. They thought this was a miracle. The arm of the man
who had actually pushed me was now paralyzed, and he asked a few of
the disciples to massage it, to bring it back to life, but it was still paralyzed.
When he asked me to try, I seized it, yanked it viciously, bit it and the
arm became normal. They realized this was Allah's business, mysterious,
hidden business.

Things like this happened again and again. Whatever I said would
happen did happen, even if the guru said it would not. If the guru said to
someone who came to see him, "You are going to die now, your time is
ending," I would interrupt. "No, he will not die, God will protect him,"
and the person would not die; if he did, he would come back to life as
soon as the relatives started to wail. The guru's word had him die, but
with mine he was restored to life again.

Finally the guru himself pushed me down a well, but God saved me
from it and the guru's hands were paralyzed. He was really a very exalted
sheikh, actually a saint, yet jealousy and pride overtook him: as the
arrogance of 'I' came in, he was lost. When I came back to the ashram
after I escaped from the well, the guru was describing a dream to his
disciples. "In my vision I saw a huge uprooted tree, its two main branches
broken off. It had been pulled out by a violent storm, hurled into pitch
blackness and tossed about in the dark. A fire erupted in that terrible

darkness, burning the tree to a crisp." He asked the disciples if they could explain this vision, and they took to their books trying to offer interpretations which made no sense.

I said, "I'll give you an explanation of the dream. You are our guru, yet your heart has changed, your state has changed. This means you will be tossed about by 'Izrā'īl, the angel of death ☺. Even though you resembled a tree, giving comfort and shade to everyone, that state came to an end. The angel 'Izrā'īl ☺ will toss you around now; you are about to leave this world."

I continued, "I have also had a vision. Let me tell you about it. There was a tree, one genuine tree of truth for the whole world. A green parrot came to sit on that tree. When the parrot started flying over the top of the tree it changed into a dove and flew to another tree close by, a tree with vicious thorns where flocks of crows lived. They came from every branch of the tree when they saw the dove, attacking it mercilessly, circling around again and again, pecking at it, biting the dove. The agony the dove endured cannot be described. It flew here and there, desperately trying to hide among the branches of the trees, but its thorns pierced it, there was no place to hide.

"Noticing the agony of the dove, I changed myself into a parrot and flew out to save it. The crows attacked me, but I changed into the form of light and in this form I rescued the dove. As I took the dove in my hand, a light came from my hand. By means of this light I could see that all the crows had been burned up. Then I told the dove, 'You should not have come to live here among the crows; you are so badly injured you will not recover. You went to that tree where you became entangled among the crows. Because you did not stay in your proper place your life is over, your life has now come to an end.' I watched the dove, held it and saw its soul leave the body as I encased it in light, sending it to heaven. The soul of the dove traveled away in the form of light."

I told my dream to the guru, whose hands were paralyzed, saying, "I believe this dream, this treasure, is about you. At first you were like God's parrot who would convey His sound. At that time you had no language of your own. The parrot could attract the sound of God and transmit it, saying only the words of God. Because you did not have that 'I' within you, you were a vehicle for God's sound, but then the evil of the world entered you. Envy, arrogance and thoughts of the world came in, the arrogance of 'I' came in and you became a dove. You flew to the *hum* of creation, you heard the *hum, hum, hum,* the sound of creation, went to that place of *hum* and became something else. The crows belong to satan. Wherever you flew you found only the crows who came to kill you. You lost your position and your state.

"Because I could change myself into a parrot who transmits the sound of God, I was able to come to your place; perhaps I will replace you because you changed. Just as you were saved from the crows when I rescued you from all your difficulties, you were also saved from satan and his qualities. Because you had the form of light again, you received the *daulat,* the treasure of God's wealth. Because you ascended in that cage of light, God will accept you, He has accepted you. This is the vision I saw and this is its meaning."

Everyone embraced me, kissing my hands and my feet, and the guru said, "God has given my *daulat* to you. Now death is drawing near me, my arms are paralyzed. It must be your hands that lift me up for burial, then you have to be sheikh to these sixty-three students."

My sheikh regained the use of his arms and died. I buried him with my own hands and became the sheikh. Although I was the youngest of the sixty-three, within a month they had received light. Some of them had been there for thirty or forty years. Until then they had not received that *daulat,* that treasure, but within a month they acquired it and were able to fly. I left them to travel the world.

I was about twenty-four or twenty-five years old when I joined the Zabūr, Hindu religion to learn who God is. They gave me many titles, but I left to join Jabrāt, the Hanal or Zoroastrian religion where I also received many titles, then I left them for the Injīl or Christian religion. They gave me many titles too, yet I went on to Furqān, the religion of Islam where they also gave me many titles. No one gave me a title that let me see God. I received status, food and physical comforts, studied the Purānas which are the Hindu scriptures, the Bible and the Qur'an. Then I understood that the power to realize God does not lie with these outer examples. The truth is found inside, and I went within myself to learn about it.

My children, if you go within yourself to study, if you try to tell the truth from the inside, the world will never accept you, no one will accept you. Illusion, intellect, desire, blood ties, even the earth will not accept you. You will become tired, and when you are tired everyone opposes you, your food, your thoughts, your vision, your body, your brothers and sisters, your religion and race, your studies and titles all turn against you. You have to keep running farther away, and as you flee this is a sign you are leaving the world and approaching God. When everyone else says they cannot accept you, He will accept you, He will give you happiness. During this flight you will fly without ties, without relatives, wives, children, brothers or sisters; you will be alone with God who will accept you. When you die within Him, when you surrender everything to Him, no one exists but God. You do not possess anything. God alone exists, only God's history exists, you have no history of your own. There is no other experience, there is no one else to praise, no one to blame. You must understand that only God will accept you because you must become God's history.

This is my experience. My history contains so many experiences, and I cannot say if I have wisdom or not, I cannot say if I am a man or a beast, I cannot say if I am a monkey or a man. I do know I am just a small ant man, I know with certainty I am a small ant man, but I cannot say I have wisdom. I have experience, I have absolute certitude in God. I do know that He is amazing, a great mystery, and that He alone never changes.

My dear, dear children, please understand this. Go within and cut your own path. There is much more to my history. It is a long story, a thing of wonder, but I am reluctant to tell it, I do not care to reveal it. You cannot assess me accurately. If a doctor tries to examine me he is unable to understand my body, it is a mystery. My heart is a mystery, my breath is a mystery, my bones and nerves are mysteries, my head and my speech are mysteries. I cannot be analyzed. Even when I go to buy a pair of slippers my feet do not fit the slippers of this world. That is just the way it is. I am different from you.

In the family of man, my history is discarded. I have merely told you a tiny dot because I do not care to reveal more. If you choose to stay here and learn just this much of my story it will be good for you. I am a small ant man now. May the children realize this and learn from it.

Many people have asked me to reveal my full history. I told them only that I have lived in Egypt and Iran, in Jerusalem and India, and once I was in the mountains of China, now I am in Ceylon. Elsewhere I stayed in a jungle among the monkeys. I have been to many, many places. This is my Purāna, my history. To understand it you must look from within because what you see now with *your* eyes is wrong; when I look at what you know with *my* eyes it appears wrong. I can interpret much from the things you have studied, yet you cannot see what I observe. What I see appears astonishing to you, and what you see appears astonishing to me, so what can we do?

Come inside and look with my eyes, or else I must look with yours. If you want to accept me, you have to put your eyes inside mine, then I can say, "Yes, I see as you see." I have seen what you see now before, but you have not yet seen what I see now. That is the difference, a great difference. You have the eyes I once had, but you have not yet acquired the eyes I see with now. I see that what you look at is false, that what I see is the truth. Still, because of the way you see now, I cannot say that what you see is wrong, yet when you are in my state you will understand the difference.

May God protect us, may He give us His grace, may He forgive us. O God, beloved Allah, grant us Your sight, Your vision. Please bestow Your eyes of grace on us and grant Your protection. *Āmīn, āmīn, āmīn,* O protector, please help us, *āmīn.*

December 9, 1973

6 | THE DIVINE ASSEMBLY

During my search for God in this world I spent twenty-one years on the first level, the state of *sharī'at*. I went looking for God in temples, churches and mosques, going without food, drink or sleep for twenty-one years. All through these years I met many priests, so-called swamis and so-called yogis, but my experience with them made it clear to me that what they said resembled truth without salt, it was tasteless. When I asked them if they had seen God they could not describe Him, their words had no taste. They told me the only way to see God was to meditate, and so I climbed a hill in the jungle, sat down under a tree, closed my eyes and spent forty-one years meditating. Although I never saw God during those forty-one years of meditation, I saw many things, glitters, lights and other astonishing marvels here in this world. Whenever I held such things up to the weapon my guru had given me, they would burn up and disappear.

I met so many deities, swamis and holy men in my search for God who would seek my help, while they were unable to offer any help to me. They would ask for my protection, they would beg me not to destroy them. Because there was no one who could give me what I wanted, I retired to the Himalayas for twelve years. There on top of a mountain I stood on one leg, touching an icicle which was rather like the root of a tree. I stood on that leg for twelve years, hoping to see God. If you were to try standing in this yoga posture you would not even be able to twist your body into this position.

When I had stood there for twelve years I woke up to find myself encased in ice and surrounded by dense fog. I used the weapon the guru had given me to break through the ice that covered me, then I saw an amazing scene. I saw many people, some who had been there for a long time, some who were standing on two feet, some who were sleeping and a few who had just been resting there for several years. Most of the people who had come there could not endure it, they left after awhile. I also saw dead people scattered all around me, some whose flesh and hearts were gone, some who were mere skeletons. They were the people who had come to practice yoga, but they were dead. Speaking to my own mind I said, "Now my mind, you have wasted my time. I have wasted seventy years trying to find God, yet I have not heard His sound, His voice or His resonance. We have both wasted our time, my mind, and these people have also wasted theirs and have perished in the process. God is not here, I must search farther," and I climbed down from there.

Then I heard a voice and held up the weapon my guru had given me; when I did this I heard a sound like a chant, not a magic chant, not a deceptive chant. This was the moment my heart received divine wisdom. I was lit with divine wisdom, I was light and saw everything, everything in existence. All the mysteries of God were revealed to me. Realizing His mystery and the secrets of His creation, I saw God Himself as a divine, brilliant Effulgence.

This was the stage at which I became a teacher in all four religions, trying hard to learn the meaning of these religions. From each of the four I selected sixty people who had reached very high states of luminous wisdom, and I became their teacher, enlightening them with deeper wisdom. I met them in their different religions, in their temples, churches and mosques, giving them the understanding of God's divine truth. I taught them the truth and reality of God which they were searching for. These people are still alive, they are not dead. They might have discarded their physical bodies, but they are alive although hidden. They might have become immortal.

These beings form an assembly which rules this earth. Just as there is a Congress in this country, these people form a congress of God, an assembly of God, and as the Congress in this country consists of a Senate and a House of Representatives, this Divine Assembly, which has many saints, is also divided into different houses of responsibility. Certain parts of the Divine Assembly are in charge of disease, how it is caused, why it is caused. Another part of the assembly is responsible for the production and distribution of food, another group is responsible for the propagation of knowledge and wisdom, still another group, the messengers of God, the *gnānis* and saints bring messages from God to this world. They come to the mountaintops to look after the physical and spiritual needs of people. Others are saints who descend to the world to conduct the affairs of the world; this is the way the world is run.

Whoever gives up the body to enter the realm of wisdom enters this congress, this Divine Assembly of God, conducting the affairs of all the eighteen thousand universes. The assembly is responsible for rain, how and where it comes, how it is controlled; they are responsible for food, who grows it, where it is grown, how it is distributed; they watch over disease, famine, plagues and pestilence, how they come, how they are controlled. All aspects of life are conducted by those beings who make up this assembly which also has certain divine angels: Jibrīl or Gabriel, Mīkā'īl or Michael, 'Izrā'īl or the angel of death, Isrāfīl or Raphael, Munkar and Nakīr, Raqīb and 'Atīd, may the peace of God be with all of them. These angels bring the commandments of God to the assembly for discussion, and once the issues are discussed, the decisions are put into effect.

I too have a connection to this assembly. I was made the head of it, the sheikh of this assembly. It is not something I wanted or accepted, but it has been bestowed upon me. Be that as it may, I do not care to discuss it further, let us talk about something else.

My beloved children, over the past four hundred years no one from the world has joined this assembly, and the reason I have come to the world during the past hundred years is to enlist members for it. During the course of my mission in this world I brought with me and distributed enough things to fill a ship so big it could hold millions of smaller ships. This is how much I have brought here and given out during my mission, yet during this last hundred years only sixteen-and-a-half people have become truly human. In my hundred years here I have been able to transform only sixteen-and-a-half people into true human beings. How many millions of people there are on this earth, nevertheless of all the millions, only these few have accepted what I have to offer. Some want what I have on my ship, except that when they come to me, they have such a huge load on their own ship they cannot accommodate what I give them.

No one seems to be ready to accept what I brought; instead, everyone tries to load me down with the things they already have, they try to sell me their things, although I cannot buy what they want to sell. Even though some people have a desire or an intention to accept what I am offering, their storehouse is full, and there is no room for what I want to give them. When they reach out to take it, they drop it as they realize they cannot store it. Some say, "Show me your God, show me the God you are talking about. We have a god we can see. Look Bawa, look at this god we have," and they show me their dog god, their Krishna or whatever god they have. They say, "Bawa, you talk about an invisible God, where is your God?"

I answer, "Even though you can see your god, can you talk to it, will it talk to you?"

They reply, "No, we cannot talk to it, but at least we can see it." All they want is something they can see with their physical eyes. Then they ask again, "Where is this God you are talking about?"

I reply, "He is within you, He is within me, He is here, He is there, He is everywhere. If you want Him you must contain Him within a certain, specific vessel. Look here, take this light I am giving you. This light is a priceless diamond. Its worth is beyond estimate. If you hold up this light you can see where God is. As soon as this diamond of light focuses on Him it beams out its messages immediately. You cannot see God without the power of this light."

"Where is this light?" they ask, "Show us this light, show us your God." But when I try to do that, I notice they bring four different types of containers to hold what I am trying to give them. The first vessel is a strainer, much like the fiber mesh of a coconut tree, the second container resembles a buffalo, the third seems to be a broken pot and the fourth resembles a swan. Everyone who comes brings one of these four containers to hold what I am offering.

When I tell them, "God is a divine nectar whose exquisite taste you will never tire of," when I invite them to drink this divine honey, and when I hold it out to them, trying to pour it into them, their vessel does not hold it. To those who come with the mind of a strainer I say, "Come here child, here is the honey, here is the nectar." But when I pour it into them the honey spills through it; only the dross, the dirt, is left behind.

Then when they look at it they say, "What's this? I see only garbage here!" and they leave.

Next come those who have minds like a broken pot. I say, "Here, hold this, drink it." I pour the nectar into their pot, they take a few steps, look into the pot and find it empty.

Everything I pour falls through the holes of the pot. This broken pot of the lower mind which has no determination cannot hold it. Then they scold me, "Where is this thing you have been telling us about? I cannot see it, you are mistaken, you have not really seen God," and they leave.

Now those with the mind of a buffalo arrive. I point to the ocean of divine nectar, the lake of exquisite clear water, urging them to drink its essence, but instead of walking along the lakeshore and drinking carefully at the shore, they wade out to the middle, jumping up and down, churning up mud, dirtying all the water. They come back from the middle of the lake and ask, "Where is this clean water you talk about, where is that exquisite taste? All we can see is dirt!" They are the ones who dirty the water and they are the ones who come back to ask the question. They take the first three steps of ascending consciousness, *sariyai, kiriyai* and *yōgam,* disturbing the purity of that divine nectar with these three steps. They also leave.

The fourth kind of person comes like a certain swan, a beautiful bird, pure white in color with a long beak. This particular swan, they say, is hard to find in the world. If you mix water and milk together, this bird dips its beak in and strains out the milk, leaving the water behind. It has the integrity and the ability to distinguish milk from water. Those who arrive like this swan are able to discriminate the worldly from the divine. They carefully extract the divine, leaving illusion behind. In the guru's words and in whatever is in your own mind and wisdom, there is a mixture of pure milk and water. Whoever can make the distinction between the two and take into himself the essence of purity, the essence of truth, has reached the station of a *gnāni,* a divinely wise being.

Only someone who has the discriminating ability to separate reality from unreality can see himself or herself, see God and merge with Him. That person alone is able to see the truth, to understand illusion. He sees his own life, he sees the lives of others and can communicate with all of them. He can hear the different prayers and meditations of various beings on earth, he understands the nature of these prayers, these meditations, he hears the sounds coming from their prayers. He is able to tune his ears to the sounds of angels and heavenly beings, to understand their prayers and meditations. He can also tune his ear to hear the voice of God coming from within himself. Although most people see things with two eyes, this divinely wise being sees with each pore of his skin. Each pore is an eye he can see with. He has billions of pores supercharged with divine light, and these pores see all around him, behind, in front, on all sides. He sees heaven, earth and everything, everything in existence. He sees everything clearly, in totality. Not a single living being is missed by these eyes because each hair follicle, each pore on the skin is an eye.

When you charge yourself with the battery of wisdom each pore is lit with light, like a light bulb. If all these lights are switched on the whole city is complete light. You are like the sun, always bright, never night, a state in which there is no day and night, it is always day. Precious children, may God grant you that kind of wisdom. Many of you come here asking me to give you what I have, but if you bring these things of yours with you, there is no room for what I have to give. Drop these things. There is no room in your storehouse for them. Come empty and openhanded, then you can store whatever I give you. May you attain this kind of wisdom. *Āmīn.*

January 9, 1972

7 | THE ROCKY MOUNTAIN

In *arwāh,* the world of souls, God gave peace to all living things, but they forgot this peace when they came here to this world. May that same peace emerge within all of them again, and may I also have that peace. May that peace be within us all, all my children, all my brothers and sisters. May we all have that peace.

Perhaps I can tell you a few incidents from my life, my history. During my life I searched to find where, when and how I could find peace, serenity, tranquility and equality. The world said I would find it here, there, in that tree, this philosophy, that religion, in this cave or on that mountain. Each person or group in turn said I would find peace in all those different places, and so I went to each one of them searching for peace. They said if I meditated I would find peace, they said if I chanted mantras I would have peace, then they said if I performed miracles I would have everything. They said, "If you experience the different features of these miracles you will find peace."

I tried each and every thing, one by one, but I did not find peace. I studied all the religions, Zabūr, that is Hinduism, Jabrāt or fire worship, Injīl, a name for Christianity, and Furqān, another name for Islam. I tried to find peace in whatever they talked about.

Certain religious leaders, some *ambiyā'* or messengers and some gurus said I had to travel the path of religion, study the religions. I did that. Others said, "You can't find peace there, go to the jungle." But wherever I looked I saw fighting, murder, separation and a sense of differences. Wherever I looked that is what I saw, not a single race or religion without fighting, without murder. At last I said, "O this is hopeless, where can I go, what religion can I turn to, where can I go?" When I looked at the sea I saw one creature eating another, creatures fighting with each other, the bigger ones eating the smaller ones. When I went to the jungle it was the same, when I went to the city they were also fighting and when I went to the religions there was the same fighting in each religion. Within each race

I found similar fighting too. Even among members of the same race they fought and devoured each other.

Then a *gnāni,* a wise man said, "Are you searching for peace? Go to a cave high up in a mountain, sit there, meditate, worship and pray, then you will find peace."

I said, "O do you think so? All right, I will go." I went there, to a tall mountain, sat and prayed a long while. Five years, six years, eight years, ten years went by, but when I used my eyes I still found it was all fighting. In the jungle, in the city, everyone was fighting, there was murder everywhere. I said, "What does this mean? There is no place where God is not, yet there is no place without fighting and murder, no place without sin. Where will I find peace now, where can I go?" I thought, "I have been sitting in this place for ten years and it is no different here."

As I was having these thoughts, the rocky mountain I was sitting on began to speak, "They are all stone-hearted, each of them murdering someone else." The rocky mountain said, "O man, come here." Then it asked, "Where do you think you are? Are you sitting inside this cave on the mountain, are you meditating inside this rocky mountain cave? You think you are sitting here meditating to find peace, but you have grown a rocky mountain inside yourself harder than this mountain on the outside. There is a rocky mountain you have grown inside yourself where you have nurtured arrogance, you have nurtured pride, yet you call that peace and equality. You keep searching for peace for yourself, you keep searching for tranquility for yourself, you are searching for serenity and quiet for yourself. But this rock mountain you are growing inside you is an immense cave. You are not sitting inside me, you are sitting in the cave you have made for yourself. Whatever you have grown inside yourself is the cave you are sitting in. You are in the cave you have built yourself, but you say you are sitting in a rocky mountain cave.

"First break down that rocky mountain you have inside you, break down that karma, arrogance, selfishness and pride which are all inside, break them down. This rocky mountain of the world is inside you; first break that down. You are sitting beneath the mountain of the world: that world and that rocky mountain are inside you, and you are sitting there inside them. You have pride, conceit, your name, your fame, your title and your miracles, and in the middle of all this you keep trying to find peace and serenity.

"But these treacherous weapons, the weapons of murder, are inside you. These weapons which cause all the trouble are still inside you. If you can throw away this world and these weapons, then you will discover where peace and tranquility are, you will discover where justice and honesty are, you will discover the truth telling you where human beings live, where animals live.

"O man, first become a true human being. If you become a true human being all living things will bow down before you. If you become God all living things will worship you. If you become a *gnāni,* a wise human being, you will be something peaceful for all living things. You will be a source of peace for all living things. If you become truth you will be food for everyone, and all your words will create peace. If you become justice you will bring unity and peace to the wisdom of others. If you find all this within yourself you will know the kingdom of heaven within your own self, you will have the kingdom of God inside. Then the kingdom of the world and illusion, the kingdom of hell will disappear for you, and when they leave, you will find peace.

"You will also find that everyone is your brother or sister, alive in that one place in your heart. In this light of purity which is your heart, in this light of the soul you will find all your brothers and sisters living in that kingdom. You will find everyone in that kingdom of *gnānam,* of divine wisdom, in that kingdom of your Father, that kingdom of the soul, that kingdom of God.

"Yet without throwing away the world and these illusions, you sit here on this rocky mountain and say you have meditated for ten years. You say you have not seen anything. You are fifty years old. For fifty years you have been sitting on this mountain within you, and you have only sat on this outer mountain for ten years. Whoever it was who went into that mountain inside never came out, never escaped from it. Come out from that rocky mountain of the world and find peace and tranquility. As long as you do not break up this mountain and throw it away, you will not find peace.

"You have four sections within you. You have to cross over the path of earth where you are assaulted by gales and storms. Then there is the sea of life. You have to cross over the ocean of water. Then the winds and storms of the air beat you down, storms which can make the land a sea and the sea into land. You have to cross over this sea of storms and gales until you come to fire. All your thoughts and everything you see are the fires that can destroy other beings, they can burn other people. Your thoughts, your intentions, what you see, these are the things that can kill others and destroy them. These spirits, these words can kill, they can destroy or cause pain and suffering to others.

"These four sections are there inside you, and you have to throw them away, overcome them. There is a fifth thing, torpor, ether or outer space. You can be enchanted by illusion, by maya, by what you see, and you can make others feel the fascination of these illusory desires. The earth is your body, water is the life composed by the liquid part of your body, air consists of the thoughts and intentions in your body, the spirits, fire is the strong heat which comes from each feeling of anger, jealousy or pride, feelings which attack and hurt others and ether is torpor, the selfishness which destroys your life. You have to overcome these five, you have to go beyond these five.

"These five things take five forms, and they also take the form of five religions. As long as you do not understand this and overcome them, you suffer. Understand this, know it and emerge from these five. As long as you do not, you cannot cross over the world and overcome it, you cannot find peace. You must understand these five, know them and go beyond. Only then will you find peace. Understand them, discover what the religions are, what prayer is, what truth is, who you are, who God is, what peace is, what justice is, what conscience is, what life is and who your family is. Discover whether we are one or many. Where did the six kinds of life come from, are they within me or do they exist on the outside in others? Earth life, fire life, water life, air life, ether life, light life—are they inside me or do they live somewhere else?

"Investigate this and you will understand that the water lives are inside you, germs and viruses which live in water are within you. Next are the lives that live in the air and lives that live in the earth which exist as atoms, as viruses, as cells. What was inside you, God brings outside and keeps it outside. The fish and the other sea creatures, the water beings of the sea and the animals in the jungle are all living things within you. These six kinds of life which are inside you are also visible on the outside.

"What exists on the inside takes form on the outside, what exists on the outside is found within. You must understand this. Once you understand this, you will not kill those lives that come from inside you. Once you know these lives came from you, you will not kill them, you will not eat them because they are part of you. Instead, you will send them to their respective sections to let them develop there. You will let them go to their respective places and you will escape. Then you will have less weight inside you, the world will be less, you will be free of the world. Send everything from the air, from your *nafs*, your base desires, back to the air. Send everything that lives in fire back to the fire, send those qualities to the fire. Give back to God what lives in God and send the things that live in illusion to illusion. Then you who came from God can go back to God, you will live in Him. Then you can find peace. First go back. Understand this, learn this and you will find peace."

This is what the rocky mountain said, then continued, "You did not understand that. Now I am only a stone, but you are a stone made of clay; I am a rocky stone, you are a clay stone. At least I can be used for something while you are made of clay and cannot be used for anything. I can be used to build bridges or houses, but you are a soft lump of clay which cannot be used for anything. If you do not understand that, you will not be of use to the world or to God, you will not serve any good purpose.

"First learn to be a true man. There is no use just sitting here. You are not sitting inside me, you are sitting in the rocky mountain within yourself, you are sitting in the cave of your arrogance, karma and illusion. Now go, understand about those caves. The jungle is inside you, the city is inside you, the mountain is inside you, the animals are all inside you. Now go, hunt all this down, discover it and complete that understanding. Then you will find peace."

This is what the rocky mountain told me. May we all undertake to understand this. I give you my love, my love you. I did hear what the rocky mountain said and set about studying these things, one by one, all over again. I did my research into these areas, what happens in the earth, in water, the grass, the insects, the birds, the monkeys, what they do, what kind of unity they have. I looked at reptiles and ants, observing what they were doing. I wandered around wondering where I could find peace.

The mountain had told me to search and study in the religions; so I went to the religions. There I found four people, a thief, a madman, a drunk and a swami or *gnāni*, all sitting around under a tree. They sat there with their beards and mustaches, each talking in his own language saying ah, ooh or something else in his own tongue. I had the thought, "These are four *gnānis*, four wise men from the four religions, perhaps I can learn something from them." I went over to the tree and stood there watching. The swami who was a holy man had a Bible, the drunk had an old book, one of the Purānas, the Hindu scriptures, the madman held a piece of paper and the thief had a bag with a pair of scissors and some other instruments. The thief kept looking at the things in his bag which he held as if it were a little book, something he kept reading nonstop.

Since these four individuals happened to be there, I thought I should stay around to see what went on. They all started staring at each other and began to yell, they began to fight. As the four men started to fight passersby noticed, "O the four swamis are fighting," and a great crowd gathered to watch. I thought, "If I get involved in this I might have to fight with them," so I decided to keep out of it and just observe what went on.

Now the four of them stood up to walk away, the drunk stumbling this way and that, spitting and making different noises, the madman making funny noises too. The *gnāni* was crazy; even though he was called a *gnāni*, he had a kind of madness too. They were all crazy, the thief was crazy, the madman was crazy, the swami was crazy and the drunk was crazy. The swami was acting strangely, doing this and that, making various signs, talking to someone. He held up the Bible then raised his hand, talking to someone in the sky. The drunk stumbled around walking everywhere, apparently looking for something, picking up anything he thought might be valuable. He kept looking at the paper in his hand. This man's madness was an obsession for money. He started preparing his accounts, writing checks, "The train is mine, the shop is mine, the world is mine," he was counting, writing it all down saying, "They're all mine." It was the desire for money that drove the drunk mad.

The madman had an obsession for a certain woman. Thinking a photograph of the woman was on a piece of paper, he picked it up and started kissing it, holding it to his heart and then embracing it. All four were going through performances in their own deluded way. The thief was obsessed with miracles, the drunk was obsessed with money, the swami holding the Bible talked in a crazy way, and the madman was obsessed with women.

The thief, was also a philosopher who believed in miracles. He had a pair of scissors. He held the scissors to a dry leaf and said, "O leaf, you were so beautiful when you first came here, you had such a lovely color, but now you are dry and tomorrow you will be dust." He started to cut it up saying, "Now you are finished, you are nothing." Then he bent over, "Tomorrow I will be dust too; you will become dust and I will also be dust. There's no point in any of this, what can we do?" He looked up, he looked down, he picked up a leaf. The madman held up a paper looking for the picture of a woman. The drunkard was looking for money. The swami holding a Bible talked to someone up above saying, "I am great, I am coming there too."

The four of them were walking along the same road, not letting anyone else pass them by, all acting the same way. Each had a different obsession, but they were acting the same way; one was obsessed with a woman, one with money, one with philosophy and one with spiritual knowledge. Each of them had a dominating thought which had made him insane.

Then I heard a sound, "Do you understand? Do you see these four people, do you understand them? This is what the religions are like. Understand this; it is madness. They all have a certain reason for their madness, something happened in their lives and they went mad. This is what is called religion. Do you understand that?

"However, there is a true religion which comes from God's decree, from something He commanded. You must learn this from within. The other is seen on the outside. Find out what is inside and learn it with clarity. This is the real religion. To understand the words of God within that religion is the truth. When you find this truth you will find peace, and that peace is God. Then the unity you see in this place is the unity of God's kingdom. This is the kingdom of peace where you accept everyone as if they were your own. You think of all living things as your own life, and see all lives as your own. This is peace. The love that comes when you think of all lives as your own is paradise, the kingdom of God.

"Understanding that state is prayer. Churn everything and extract peace from it. This is the way to have peace. Paradise is God, man and the truth living together. Only when this state is established within you do you find peace, and then the peace of all living things is your peace and ease, the peace of all lives is the wealth, the joy of your life. When you understand this state, that is wisdom, the state of love, the state of God's qualities. As long as you fail to know this or understand it, you do not have peace in your life. You have the suffering of hell, you have mental pain. You suffer and experience torture in life and die an undying death. Your life goes on but you are not dead, you die inch by inch. This is a terrible disease which tortures you. Think about it. When you understand this, when you realize this you will recognize that the peace of others is your peace.

"You will see the lives of others within yourself, and the joy in their lives will be your joy. You will know God's joy and taste it little by little. Until you know this, you are like these madmen, each with a different reason for his madness. Each man has a reason, a source, of his madness. Everyone is walking along the same road but each with his own insanity.

"You must have the clarity to find that one treasure, God, Allah; take the truth, wisdom and meaning from each thing, one by one. On that day you will have your peace and the peace of others. If you do not do that you will not find peace in this world, in the kingdom of God, in the kingdom of souls, in your own life or in the kingdom of heaven.

"You can only find that peace once you have discarded everything. What remains will be God's qualities, the four virtuous qualities of modesty, reserve, sincerity and fear of wrongdoing, good conduct, *sabūr*, inner patience, *shakūr*, absolute contentment, *tawakkul-'alallāh*, trust in God, and *al-hamdu lillāh*, offering all praise to Allah. Just as ghee can be churned and extracted from milk, churn yourself and extract these qualities. You can make ghee from milk step by step, then when you melt the ghee it is like a mirror in which you can see yourself.

"In the same way, you have to churn the five elements within you and churn your five senses with wisdom to extract *īmān*, absolute faith, and the truth that is God. Churn your heart with wisdom, churn the five elements, the five senses and extract the truth. Then when you melt this truth you will see that God is a mirror and that you are the form seen in that mirror. God is the mirror in which you see your form. Once you churn the heart, your beauty and form are seen there in that mirror, and within that beauty you see into each and every thing in existence. You will see that peace. This is what you have to find, yet as long as you study the religions without knowing that, you will not reach the station of truth. Religions are practiced for many different reasons, but God has said just one word. The essence, the resplendence in all the religions is just one point.

"God's essence, His *rahmat*, His grace or mercy, rises up step by step. First it was in the earth, then it grew larger and it grew again. Then it rose up, it stretched and came up, it ascended, it grew and then it emerged. God's *rahmat* grew and grew and grew in the religions too, until finally it emerged. First it grows in the religions, then it grows in man and becomes God. You must go through the four religions, extract the truth from them, learn about *insān*, a human being, and extract what is within him; in this you can find the truth. Step by step His *rahmat* grows. God's word grows and flourishes."

These are the words given to me many, many years ago, and then wherever I went, I found all these madmen. Whichever road I traveled I found madness, the kind of madness stemming from different thoughts. They all had a certain stubbornness or obstinacy about a particular thing, either an obsession about color, race, religion or any kind of difference. They all had something, yet if they lost their money or had a bout of diarrhea, the madness would leave. No one accepts you if you have no money. The religions will not accept you. As long as you have physical strength, physical beauty, money, a home, property, only then do they accept you. If you have something they accept you, but if you do not have anything they find useful they will not accept you. They accept you because they can gain something from you; otherwise they will not accept you.

This is what happens in the world. Only if you churn yourself to extract everything about man and God, only if you collect the truth yourself are you able to understand it. That is the truth. This means your wisdom has to penetrate everything to find clarity with *īmān*, with absolute faith. To do this you need faith, certitude, determination and *īmān*, faith in God. You must also have the qualities of *sabūr*, inner patience, *shakūr*, absolute contentment, *tawakkul-'alallāh*, trust in God, and *al-hamdu lillāh*, offering all praise to God. You need wisdom, the wisdom to learn how to acquire these qualities, how to know these things and find clarity.

Open your heart! You have to open your heart, discard this *dunyā*, this world, and remove all the veils of the world. Keep God and His kingdom within yourself, keep God's justice within you. You must know today the judgment God will pass on you tomorrow. Know your faults and try to correct them. Before He raises you on Judgment Day, before He passes judgment on you, judge yourself while you are here. Would that not be a good thing to do? Before there is an inquiry in the hereafter about the good and the bad you have done, would it not be a good idea to understand the good and the bad you have been responsible for while you were here? Before you are judged ready for heaven or hell in the hereafter, should you not recognize the good things and the bad things you actually do here now, and ever after avoid evil, accept the good and live on in those good qualities?

If you investigate yourself, you can discover where you are and learn what is good. If you have that judgment here instead of there, later on you will not be found guilty because this is the same inquiry which takes place afterwards. Throw away the evil, the sin which stems from each thought, each look, each intention, and keep just the ones that are good and use them. Then sin will not touch you, evil will not appear. If you go on doing this throughout your life, if you make this judgment on yourself during your life, you build your own heaven and have the right to be one with your Father. Recognize both the sound and the light of your Father in your actions. Keep seeing this, keep checking this during your life and you will never separate from your Father in this world or the hereafter. This is peace, and understanding this is what you have to learn.

Everyone came here to learn this. Think about it. Everything you see is a guru. All God's creations, all the creatures made by the Creator are here for you to study the good and the bad, to have clarity about the things that are good and the things that are bad, to know what truth is, what falsehood is, to know what is good, what is evil, what food is good, what food is bad. Some things are poisonous and some things are not. There are good human beings and bad human beings, good animals and bad animals. You have to learn how to understand all this.

I give you my love, my precious children. These words given to me during my life are the words I am telling you now. This is the way to find clarity in your life. Instead of waiting for tomorrow's Judgment Day, correct yourself, judge yourself while you are still alive. The courthouse, God's house, heaven and hell are all within you. God's house, the house of heaven, the house of judgment, the house of paradise, the house of hell, the house of peace are all within you, and you must know which is which. If you build the right things inwardly, you will find peace.

May you think about this. I give you my love, jeweled lights of my eyes. These are certain words given to me in the course of my experience. *As-salāmu 'alaikum,* may the peace and blessings of God be with you. *Āmīn.*

December 22, 1983

8 | WHAT BAWA MUHAIYADDEEN ☺ HEARD WHILE IN MEDITATION

During my meditation I found myself praying high up above the world somewhere, a station high above the world. I could see it beneath me. In America they show you a globe they call the world, and this is the way it appeared to me, a globe. I was praying high up above it. While I prayed every atom seemed to emerge from a certain source. Everything was silent and still until somebody touched or prodded it, then an atom would emerge. There was no place where this did not happen. As soon as a cause or basis for action was presented, the atom would project only what had already happened. While I was seated in meditation I saw this.

Suddenly the station where I was praying changed; what had been the world was split in two, and I was thrown down onto a mountain of ice. I found myself upside down seated in meditation, my hands clasped together, but my head was down and my feet were up. The place I was in resembled a grave, yet the space was not oppressive, it seemed open, but I could not speak. I stayed in this state for about an hour, looking at all the things that had happened before, all the times I had been here, what I did earlier. My life had not left me although my body had turned into a block of glistening ice which shone like crystal, like a glistening palace of ice. My body still had life, and within it I could see every thought emerging as a *shakthi*, an energy. The *rūh*, the soul, had not departed, and I could see myself speaking.

I was at the center of a sound that came from everywhere. All the creations and all they had done came back to my memory. Everything spoke, telling me what it was or what it did. I would tap each thing and pour a different kind of medication on each. I found these medications created a different effect on each of them. One might cause unconsciousness, another prevent unconsciousness. Some medications exposed what had happened earlier, some medications revealed what would happen later or what came in between. Some medications took things to the brink of death.

They were all speaking about such things. Each time a certain creation was nudged by something it would relate its earlier experience. Each atom, each cell, each virus emerged to communicate with me, explaining that if you take one chemical and apply it to another, such and such an effect would occur. They explained that you can take something from one of the five elements and give it to another element, you can take something from earth and give it to fire, you can take something from the sun, from water, air or ether. As we took something from each of them and gave it to something else, certain atoms had different ways of speaking.

Then the states of the jinns, the fairies, angels and prophets were shown to me, with the meaning of each state revealed. All these things were revealed as I talked to them. The sound coming from within seemed to be a solid rocklike form, even though it was speech. It came from a state in which the body did not move or shake. No matter where anything originated, the sound emerged only when I prodded or tapped it, whether it was heat, the soul or even a stone; unless I touched it the atom would not come forth.

For that reason, if you want to analyze something, whether it is the *rūh,* the soul, or anything else, you have to prod it, you have to make contact with your wisdom before it will emerge. There are seven levels of wisdom. To investigate every point at each level of wisdom you have to make contact with it, tap or nudge it. This applies to anything you want to analyze in this world. Otherwise, a natural investigation must ripen by itself. If this natural investigation matures by itself, ripens by itself, it will fall just as ripened fruit falls naturally from a tree. Once it reaches a certain maturity it drops by itself, and in the same way, when a man's soul, his state, his prayer, his meditation, his wisdom and his investigation reach maturity, they drop by themselves. Then where do they go? They go straight to God. If that power has not been achieved, they have four hundred trillion, ten thousand spiritual qualities. Research and investigation show each different quality. Then you have to give it a particular chemical to change that quality, you have to make contact, tap it awake and give it the right chemical, whatever the research dictates.

Certain medications you give to people who are insane make them drowsy; some make them unconscious and they are not aware of their surroundings. Some medications awaken memories, things that happened before are revealed to a patient and come back to him again and again. Yet only what happened before is revealed, not what will happen. What will happen in the future, what is about to happen is not shown, nor are the four virtuous qualities of modesty, reserve, sincerity and fear of wrongdoing. Only the things that are already over are awakened. It could be love, money or whatever, these memories come back. This is what that chemical brings back, this drowsiness evokes those memories.

There is another medication which makes a person expansive, it creates hunger; another one locks a person in silence, he does not speak, he merely sits with his head bowed. This is the nature of that chemical. He might cry, he might just sit staring off into the distance or with his eyes fixed on something. His attention does not wander. Certain medications make people want to tear their hair out or pull off an arm or a leg, some chemicals make them do this.

Each chemical produces its own effect. Some make a person use filthy language, some create anger, some make a person bite or scold or curse. Each chemical has some effect, continually turning the mind upside down, always producing what happened earlier; still, these chemicals do not take the person to a place where he thinks about the life that is to come, how he should conduct that life. Chemicals keep turning him back to face the past, what happened before, what is over and done with. They do not take him to a state of clarity where he can think and plan his future. This cannot be done with chemicals.

What do you have for that, what do you use to make a person contemplate the future? With words, with wisdom and love you have to diminish wrong tendencies and take that person to another place. You have to make him want to leave the wrong place by giving certain explanations and saying, "Do this, do that, come here, look at this." You must interest him in the alternative, and while he is busy with the things you are trying to show him, you also try to divert the other influences. As understanding from this investigation arises, as he keeps on digging into each explanation and the understanding becomes correct, it will engage him. The wisdom of these qualities will attract him, the essence of these qualities or actions will attract him.

What I saw at that time, in fact, were many different kinds of analysis and research. If you reach the right state by yourself the world cannot swallow you; with the right kind of investigation different things can be understood. In that investigative state you can hear the sounds of many things. You can also send out your own sound. In this state, you are able to emit or receive sound.

I saw much more, but that is all I can remember. There were many things I saw during this meditation, things about science, the methods of science, about the chemicals or *shakthis* within things, the energies that were trying to change the world, to reduce all the good qualities, to keep your attention focused on things which happened in the past, things which were over long ago, instead of trying to consider the future and what you should do with your life.

Psychologists and scientific researchers are only concerned with what happened in the past, with women, sex, wealth or whatever occupied your attention before. But if you really investigate properly and find the right point....If a fruit matures it falls by itself. When that atom comes to fruition the fruit falls. When a pearl ripens in the oyster and is mature it loosens by itself. When every point matures in the right state it releases itself from the world, it shakes itself free of the world and falls away. Every thought shakes itself free of the world and falls away. As each quality develops to maturity, it is released and all that is left is God's power, nothing else. Everything else falls away.

I have forgotten the rest of what I saw. Is this sort of thing reported in the research and investigations of science, to be upside down in a state like a glistening crystal of ice, head down, feet up? Later on, the position was corrected, my head came up again, yet when I was first turning upside down I thought, "O it's all over, they are going to bury me in this grave." This was what I thought, but they did not, although I did think everything was finished. My form remained as it was. I could hear things and I could even send out messages. My legs and hands were not together, but extended or at my side. My body was positioned for meditation even though it was upside down, head down, signifying the way a child is positioned in the womb with its head down, feet up. When a baby is in the womb, at first the head is up and the feet are down; later, when it is ready to be born, the head goes down. It corrects itself before it comes out. When you pray you sit erect; still, if you reach the maturity, the ripeness of that, perhaps you do turn upside down and emerge the other way. This is the way it seems to me, I do not know. I really saw this and it looked so beautiful. Those were the exact words spoken to me.

Before a chick hatches from the egg it has a certain sound, a certain voice, it makes a sound inside the egg. As it pecks at the shell trying to come out, trying to crack it open, it makes that sound and the mother hen appears to help it come out. The sound the chick makes inside the egg can be heard only by the mother hen. In the same way, the sound coming from a heart filled with the tenderness of true prayer can be heard only by God. Even in your dreams, if you have a nightmare and shout, the person lying beside you will not hear it, although to the dreamer it is a terrible sound as he screams in the terror of his nightmare. Every kind of fearful, strangled sound might come from the dreamer at that time, sometimes even waking him up. Just as a person lying beside the dreamer may not hear what he shouts in his nightmare, the words that go out from your *qalb*, your inner heart, the words that go out from your wisdom are heard by God alone. Even someone beside you will not know. And as a chick makes a sound inside the egg which is music to the hen's ear, once the shell cracks and the chick comes out, the sound is quite different, it cannot ever make the same sound again.

When you are a little seed your sound is different, yet once you emerge, your sound, your life and your conduct change. A different wind blows across you, your food is different, the level of heat changes, your environment is entirely changed. When you are connected to God, when you are deep in prayer, in worship, in *dhikr* or *fikr*, the remembrance or contemplation of God, when you are in that state of connection to God, it is beautiful. If you do your prayer in the right way, with deep feeling, the sound coming from you is beautiful. Whenever you do your prayer in the right way there is a beautiful sound, but if you change, if you move away from that place of prayer and come back into the world, it is like the chick once it breaks the shell and comes out. When you go into a state of prayer your sound is different, but once you leave that prayer your sound is different. Once you leave there, the sound is like a chick's after it breaks the shell. The world surrounds you, your desires, your cravings, your hunger, many things make that sound entirely different, and then you start fighting, you quarrel about your house, your property, anything. If you reflect on all this you will realize how much subtlety there is in each of these points.

If I am a man, my children will become true men too, human beings. They will be children of wisdom, and if they are children of wisdom they will be children of God because they will have the qualities of God, they will be God's family. Then there is no fear.

In His divine words from His divine sound God told the prophets, "I created Adam who knows things even the heavenly beings do not know, Adam has the ability to know things the angels and heavenly beings are incapable of knowing."

Jinns and fairies have only thirty-six *tatthwas* or potentialities, even though they are capable of exchanging one form for another. They can change their form, they have many abilities, they can even fly, but the children of Adam ☺ know things the heavenly beings do not know. In the blink of an eye, these beings can fly all around the world and come back to where they started. They can create the world within themselves and they can cancel the world within themselves, they can throw it away. These beings are created with earth, fire, water, air and ether, five angels which form the world.

Some beings are created with fire. There are earth lives, fire lives, air lives, water lives, ether lives and then there is the life of man which is a life of light. Fire lives and light lives are different. The life of light comes from God. It has to come from God because it emerges from God, this life of an *insān*, of a true human being. The others all come from creation, from earth, fire, air and ether, but the life of light comes from God Himself.

God kept just one of His powers for Himself and gave all the other ninety-nine to the children of Adam ☺. He told the angels, "Only when a son of Adam strays does he come under your control. If he becomes weak you might be able to overcome him, but when he stays in his original state you are not his equal. If his wisdom weakens, if his faith weakens, when his wisdom, his *īmān*, his certitude, faith and trust in God are weak, then perhaps you can get the upper hand. As long as he is strong and remains in his original state, you can never conquer him. I kept only one power for Myself and gave all the other ninety-nine to the children of Adam.

"In the blink of an eye a person can go around the world once, he can throw the world away from himself or create it for himself. How does he do that? Each of you creates things inside your body. Man can create the world inside him or eliminate it, that is his state. He has the understanding to do this. In the blink of an eye he can bring the world into being in himself or eliminate it."

These are the divine words that came from Allah, words which came from Allah to His prophets. And He said more, "There is a Judgment Day. I have given everything to man. I have given everything to him and I will not investigate or punish him until that Judgment Day. I have allotted his *rizq*, his food and the water he needs. When the food and water set aside for him are finished, I will make My inquiries. I do not punish, I do not kill or hurt anyone, each individual does whatever he does to himself; I do not seek anyone out, I do not do anything to anyone. Someone who has lost his strength, who is weak in faith, falls under the control of satan, of demons or ghosts. Someone whose strength of *īmān* fails, whose faith, certitude and determination falter, this person brings destruction upon himself. To lose your faith in God is itself destruction.

"When a forest is dry you do not need a flame to make it catch fire, the forest can create a fire by itself. Similarly, the man who has gone astray has a forest in his heart which creates a fire, a fire that burns the forest inside him and burns him too. People destroy themselves; you do not need soldiers or armies to destroy people who have committed so many mistakes, they bring their own destruction upon themselves."

Now when you look at what is happening today, when you look at this world, it is the time of destruction when *insān* will destroy *insān,* man will destroy man. This is not God's trial, this is what happens when human beings turn into animals. One group becomes animals, one group becomes satan. You see this happening in the world today everywhere you look. It is very hard to find a country where there are true human beings. It seems to be the time when human beings kill each other, when human beings eat each other. This is what we see. Faith in God has been lost.

God does not destroy man, nevertheless human beings say, "I am in charge, I am a conqueror, I am a destroyer, I rule." And so man destroys man. God does not do this. You can see it with your own eyes at the present time. Just turn and look at the world, that is what you see.

You must try to escape from the state of the world. Brotherly unity, sisterly unity, you have to foster peace in your family. Sisters and brothers must live in unity, live in harmony. Sons and daughters, grandsons and granddaughters, neighbors, those born with you, may you all live in a state of *shānti,* of peace, a state of unity. May you all come together in unity and march to your Father's kingdom. May you bring that state of peace and tranquility to your heart.

Once you die and are laid in the grave, none of your relatives go with you, none of the members of your race go with you. They just leave you there. What takes you beyond the grave is the good and the bad you were responsible for before you died. If you have not done anything good in this life, you will not have a companion to take with you later. If you do not have true love you cannot have true unity, and this is the reason you cannot proceed beyond. You need help to go beyond the grave, and that help consists of the good actions, good thoughts and the help you offer to others while you are here. Even though you might have done evil, these are things that can liberate you, these are things that are vital for your journey beyond the grave. Think about this.

These are the things that give you the great victory of your life, the victory that peace will bring. May you struggle hard for this. Every child, think deeply about it. *Āmīn, āmīn. As-salāmu 'alaikum.* May the peace of God be in your heart, now and always.

July 31, 1985

9 | The True Value of Experience

I farm now and because my life is dedicated to helping others, I can help many families with my work on the farm. When I first came to this farm it was jungle I had to clear, then I had to dig the earth with nothing but a spade before I could plow it and make drainage ditches. I grew rice and vegetables for the people, supplied fodder for cows and goats, I even put a fence around the land.

I have worked at many jobs. I have been a baker, a laundryman, once I worked as a slave. I have also practiced medicine. I have exorcised demons and taught divine knowledge. I have done many different jobs, yet while I was doing all this I have never failed to carry out God's commands. I do God's work, and when I leave here I will continue to do His work. I do God's work, but I also do the world's work, the world that you, my children, need. I teach only what I know and what I have experienced, only what I have learned from personal experience. If I have not profited from a particular thing, I do not teach it. Since I taste every ingredient of the food, if it is poisonous I will not offer it to you, if it has a sweet taste I will recommend it. Once I have tested, examined and discarded the wrong, poisonous things from my own experience, I give you the best tasting food.

My children, every word I utter comes from my personal experience. If I tried to offer you something I have not experienced, it would be like information found in a book, it would be of no use to you, it would be doubtful. What I give you is the wisdom and knowledge of my experience so that it will be useful to you in this world; I utter each word without any doubt. That is its taste.

I would like each of you, my children, my sons and daughters, to learn and absorb knowledge through direct personal experience. There is no other way to find God. God-man, man-God. This means if a true human being is there, God is also there, if a true human being is not there, God is not there. If a human being becomes the prince of God, that person will see the divine radiance of God because God and the true human being are in the same place, and there, at that place, the human being is a divine radiance who knows the world and everything in it. Like the sun, he can light up the whole world with the divine light he has within himself, a light which knows everything. This human being knows both day and night, he knows every limitless aspect of creation.

What you see on the outside is nothing but illusion and doubt. You need light to overcome illusion, and you can only have this light with direct experience, as I did. No one has ever given this important explanation in all four *yugas*, not in two hundred million years, but this is my personal, direct experience. My children, please reflect upon this and understand it well. It is all a dream. The only truth is what wisdom sees. May Allah help you. *Āmīn.*

November 13, 1972

10 | LIFE IN THE JUNGLE

I have inscribed my words on the ashram walls so often they are several inches thick, but they have not impressed themselves to the depth of an atom on people's hearts. Once people leave me they forget everything. If it were not for the few who are seeking the truth, I would go back to the jungle to live.

It is far superior to live in the jungle. There, lions, tigers and bears surround me at night to protect me and do service to me. In the daytime, when I sing or meditate, snakes, peacocks, birds and other beings surround me. It is a happy life in the jungle. Even though the animals cannot speak they bow their heads down and listen attentively. Elephants are thoughtful, they look at the ground, and except for a slight swaying movement they stand still, listening carefully. Then when I finally open my eyes and see them, it is such a wonderful sight!

There is always something new and wise to be learned from the animals. Some snakes listen with their hoods open, some with their hoods closed and heads bent low, as if they were bowing. There is so much truth to be learned from sights like these. You can see the power of God within them, see how it penetrates their lives.

I can look into their hearts and realize the wonder of God's power within them. How great is the power of God! There is so much to learn there, so much to learn about the power of God by looking at each and every one of the animals. Although they are unable to speak and people consider them to be unintelligent, I have not seen God's power reflected in human beings as I saw it in all the animals when I was in the jungle, there where the power of God is so evident. When I look into the hearts of these animals, I see life resonating, I see it pulsing in them. I do not see the material world in their hearts, just the power of God. The external world does not live in these hearts because animals live moment by moment, they do not worry about tomorrow's food. When they are hungry they search for the food they need right then. They do not concern themselves about killing or destroying anything for tomorrow, they do not think of planning an attack, they do not think of revenge. This means that when they hear the resonance of God it pierces their hearts like a pointed shaft. They bend low in quiet reverence when they hear that sound.

In the heart of the animal we call man however, thoughts of the world, of today, tomorrow and yesterday cloud the power of God. God's power is walled off by such thoughts, by thoughts of killing someone, of harming someone or taking revenge. These thoughts form a wall in front of God's power, and therefore His power recedes farther and farther away. The sound of God bounces off this wall of thoughts, unable to penetrate the inner depth of a man's heart, like a sound echoing off the side of a mountain. All earthly thoughts deflect this sound when it comes, preventing it from resonating inwardly.

This is the reason it is easier to live with animals in their original state than to live with an artificial animal called man. If I live with real animals they can learn from me and I can learn from them, but if I live with this artificial animal man, half-baked man like a Shaker-Maker toy, I learn only sorrow because that power has been diverted away from him. Like an echo, it does not penetrate, it cannot resonate within.

What I learned from the animals, what the animals learned from me was the power and praise of God, and this makes life in the jungle infinitely better. If you compare these animals in their original, complete state with the half-baked animal which man has become, you discover that these original animals have a magnet which attracts the power of God. Plastic man does not have this. You think of man as plastic now because he behaves as if he were stuck together and colored with pieces of plastic; he is a plastic man, just stuck together and filled with air to give him shape. If you do not pump air into him he is a shriveled scrap of plastic. Even if you fill him with air, once there is a leak he will be thrown in the trash. There is no point believing in plastic man because eventually he will be thrown away and put on a garbage truck.

When I look at these two kinds of animals, I see the most dangerous one comes in the shape of man. If you save yourself from this animal called man and go back to the original animal, you will see they have the power of God in them. If a man communes with them and learns from these animals, the subject is God's greatness. All praise belongs to God, but if you talk to plastic man you learn about everything except God, and all praise is offered to the earth and the things of the earth. Even the mention of God, the hint of God, does not enter the conversation; all praise is offered to man and the earth. And so you see, if I go back to the jungle I can think about God, I can have some rest and peace there.

You tell me which is better for me, this life with you or life in the jungle? Certainly, if someone is here who has that sense of God within him, it is worthwhile spending time with him, otherwise my time is wasted. I might just as well spend time with a piece of wood or animals in the jungle.

When a man wants to tame a monkey he does so by weaning the monkey from its natural qualities and habits, and by teaching it his own instead. He will say, "Hey monkey, turn a somersault," and the monkey will turn a somersault. Or, "Hey monkey, go over to this man and bring me that picture," and the monkey will go to the man with its hand held out to bring back the picture. Or, "O Hanumān, you monkey! Imitate me." Then the trainer will act like a cowherd and will pick up a stick and strut around. Then the monkey will imitate him. In this way, the trainer imposes new habits on the monkey to earn a living for himself. He becomes a sheikh to the monkey.

Similarly, a man with the qualities of a wild monkey must find a true sheikh and be tamed. First he must discard his own attributes, and then adopt the qualities and ideals of the sheikh. Only if he gives up his own habits can he learn the habits of the sheikh. If he does this, the sheikh can put a chain around his waist, as a monkey trainer chains a monkey, and change him. The sheikh will say, "Come here, look at God," just as if he were training a monkey. He will say, "Come, I'll show you God; now do a somersault," and he will make the earth itself turn a somersault and do all kinds of tricks. He will show this man the truth that is God. He will shake up the monkey mind and the earth, jolting them and dislodging them, and in this way the man can be free from them. The sheikh will shake up the whole world, showing that man the sham of the earth and revealing the truth that is God.

The sheikh can only uncover this truth if the man gives up his original monkey antics and accepts the teachings of the sheikh. If a man can imitate what the guru does, like a monkey, the guru will show him what to do, but if he does not copy what the guru does, there is no point wasting time with him. If a man cannot even do what a wild monkey does, what is the use of wasting time with him?

If a monkey falls accidentally from a tree and is caught by a man and then later escapes to go back to the other monkeys, they will not accept it back. They will bite the monkey and try to kill it. Or if a trainer cannot train a monkey, if it will not listen and learn the tricks it is taught, the trainer discards it, and chases it away. This is a disaster for the monkey because the other monkeys will not accept it back and the trainer will also not accept it. All it can do is wander around the jungle until some bigger animal catches and kills it.

And so if a man leaves his community behind, if he leaves the world to join the guru, then does not learn to accept the truth he has found, he will be discarded by the guru, by God and the truth; he will also be discarded by the world. If he does not learn what he needs to learn once he has left his own kind, then leaves the guru, God and his rare birth, he will be subject to many births; he will end in hell. He is not accepted by God, and he is not accepted by his own people. Death will come and he will take many births. Just as a monkey is killed if it tries to leave his trainer, neither the truth nor ignorance accepts the man who leaves his sheikh. His birth is ruined. The monkey is in limbo when it falls to the ground, it is rejected by everyone, and a man is in the same position. You must understand this clearly.

If I had a good man, a god-like man to talk to, I would not have to think this way. These thoughts would not rise, but in the absence of one such being I spend my time with a piece of wood, a cigarette or something like that. This is the way I have to spend my time, looking here and there because I have not found that person.

When I needed water in the jungle, I had to go to little ponds where sometimes there were dangerous crocodiles. As I approached they would run towards the banks of the pond, their jaws wide open and ready to devour me. But when I started walking into the water they would just stand there, watching without movement. Normally these dangerous crocodiles seize anything that moves in the water, but I would wade in up to my knees, take a drink or have a bath, and then go and stand at the edge of the pond singing a song in praise of our Creator. The crocodiles would gather around, all the animals would appear, even frogs would hop right up to the edge of the pond, all gazing intently, listening carefully, without even a ripple of water. The power of God, the sound of God, has a sweetness which pierces the heart of every living thing.

When I would end my song and walk away, perhaps to climb a tree, if I looked back a little later I could see them still there, waiting awhile, then gradually going back to their routines. There were many wonders like this to be seen in the jungle.

If a man with the qualities of God goes there, all the animals are his companions, they protect him. But if a man with animal qualities goes there he is afraid because he is just like them, and they will devour him. This is what it was like in the jungle when I lived there. My children, think about what I have said and understand the point I am making. May God protect you all. *Āmīn.*

September 15, 1972

11 | Bawa Muhaiyaddeen ☙ and the Elephants

 One hot day when I was visiting Dr. Ajwad's home at the University of Peradeniya, I decided we would take a little trip to the riverside where the air was cooler. We went by car with Dr. Ajwad, his wife Ameen, his sister Araby and a few others to the river where we saw a number of elephants, ten or twelve, some in the river. As I started to get out of the car, three elephants came quickly towards me, two off to one side of the car but one straight at me. This one at the front of the car raised its trunk and draped it across the windshield, while I sat back down in the car.

The mahout kept trying to get the elephant away from the car, but it would not move. Now everyone around me became frightened and started screaming because they thought the elephant was going to attack me. As they kept shouting with anxiety the other two elephants came up to the car, one lying down beside it, the other trying to force its head inside the window where I was sitting. When I patted it on the head this elephant started to cry, tears fell from its eyes. The mahout began to beat it, ordering the elephant to get up, but I scolded the mahout, "Don't beat this elephant, it is making a complaint. Let it state its case and then it will get up."

I listened to the elephant for some time, comforting it. By then a number of tourists had come over to the car taking pictures, and the mahout decided to capitalize on this. He tried to group the elephants scenically around the car so that the tourists would take more pictures. No one knew what I was saying to the elephant. In fact I was comforting it, "Be patient, don't cry, you have your duty to do; I have also had to go through so many difficulties. Once when I was a king with a vast kingdom, people tried to kill me for it, they tried to bury me alive just for that wealth and the land. They tried to drown me too, but God saved me. I did have so many troubles in those years, everyone tormented me, but your Creator does exist. Do the duty He created you for, go now, do your duty and know that God will take care of you. Some people want to take your picture, the world loves to do that, they love to see the outer form. They do not know who you are or who I am inwardly, they know only what they see outwardly. Go now, be at peace, I must get out of the car." When I said this the elephant got up, raised its head, trumpeted loudly in salute and bowed its head down low before me. Everyone was watching as the elephant left. You might think an elephant is unaware of God, but how else did it know enough to come to me? Even the earth is aware of the power of God.

I take care of four to five hundred sick people in Ceylon, a poor country. Many poor people come to me from a long distance away. I treat their illnesses, cure their minds, drive away their demons, feed and clothe them, I even give them the ticket money to come see me. This is the reason I have a farm, to help the poor and make enough for its upkeep. I used to get up every morning at four o'clock to go to the farm. Although sometimes I would stay there as long as forty or fifty days, usually I would come back to the ashram at night and I would have no rest, there would be crowds of people to attend to. I farmed to earn the money to feed these people. I could have told fortunes and made quantities of money. I could have told them what was in their mind, their heart or their body, but I would not do that. I labored using my body instead.

My children, a snake instinctively knows that God exists. When a tiger suddenly appears before a true man it bows down. Even a rock knows a true man. A true man does not need to advertise. Not advertising by itself is proof he is a true man. Everything has life. A drop of water is alive, a spark of fire is alive, and if we are in the right place, if we become a true human being even a blade of grass will recognize it. This is the way things are; this is the truth.

October 23, 1980

12 | THE COW

The cow in this photograph was given to me by a European man. It was a vicious cow that no one could get near. With me she would kneel down to pay homage, then when it was time to milk her, I had to stand in front of her to keep her from kicking the milkman. I would blow cigarette smoke at her to calm her down, and she would open her mouth to breathe it in. This cow gave eighteen pints of milk at each milking, however she had to be milked at exactly three in the morning and three in the afternoon.

The picture was taken in 1950, but soon after that the people who were looking after the cow while I was away sold her without asking me. The cow shed a lot of tears that day, and from the moment she left their hands, misfortune befell the people who had sold her, from that day on they had nothing but difficulties.

As for my black beard, it is only in the last three years that my beard turned white. This is due to the amount of work I do here in Ceylon. If I were in America it might turn black again.

August 9, 1972

13 | BAWA MUHAIYADDEEN ⓐ AND THE SNAKE

One day when I was praying in the jungle I had spread a small piece of cloth as a prayer mat in front of me. My prayer mat was just a small piece of blanket which I spread before me to pray the *maghrib*, the evening prayer. While I prayed a snake appeared right in front of me, but because I was focused on my prayers I did not see it. The cobra was lying flat out in front of me as I bowed down completing my first *rak'at*, the first prayer cycle. I was just about to get up to start my second *rak'at* when the snake coiled itself up right at my head, coiled itself with its hood spread in a striking position. At the first *rak'at* it had been sliding towards me in a straight line, however when I saw it during the second *rak'at* it was coiled and ready to strike.

After my first *rak'at* I had just casually noticed it stretched out, but I did not pay attention to it because my concentration was elsewhere. However, after my second *rak'at*, my second prayer cycle, when I stood up I saw it coiled with its hood spread out and ready to strike. I rose from the second *rak'at*, started the third and saw the cobra still in a striking position. I finished my three *fard* or obligatory *rak'ats*, prayed the two *sunnah*, the customary *rak'ats*, then the two *nafl* or optional *rak'ats*, seven *rak'ats*, seven prayer cycles, gave my *salāms* to the angels and recited the four verses making up the *Fātihah*. While I did all this the snake remained coiled, poised to strike, although at some point it dropped its head onto the coiled section of its body allowing me to finish all my prayers, waiting like that until I completed my prayers.

When I finished the prayers I pulled the piece of blanket that served as my prayer mat away from the snake, folded it up and asked the snake, "Where did you come from?" It spread its hood again. Then I continued, "Because I was the one praying you kept yourself from striking, but if it had been someone else, the outcome would have been entirely different. You should never appear in front of someone who is praying. If you ever see someone praying this way again, you must leave." The snake uncoiled itself and slid away.

On another occasion when I was praying, the same kind of snake presented itself in front of me. It happened in a house where no one had stayed or prayed for ten years because it was said there was a cobra inside. I had been walking along a road one day when someone complained to me there was a house with a snake inside, and I agreed to investigate. I said, "I will stay in that house today and pray there." The walls of the house were made of mud with a hole in one of them where the snake lived. At *'ishā'* prayer, the night prayer, first I prayed the four *sunnah* or customary *rak'ats,* then the four *fard* or obligatory prayers, not thinking about the snake because I was concentrating on my prayer. While I was in the middle of a prostration the snake came out of its hole and stationed itself in front of me. It was a cobra with an enormous head which waited there, motionless, while I completed a total of seventeen *rak'ats* of prayer.

Then when I finished my prayers I asked it, "Who are you?" It was a *rūhānī,* an elemental spirit which had hidden itself away as a snake in that house for about ten years. I called to the snake, "There is no point staying here, you have to leave." It shook its hood twice and I said, "Get out of here *shaitān,* you satan, or I will have to kill you, go!"

As it left it shrieked like a person, "Aaooo!" making this wailing sound. Once it had left I left, and about eight months later when I came back along that road people told me the snake was no longer in the house.

When you pray, even though a snake or anything else should appear, if you focus on anything but your prayer it is not prayer because your concentration has to be one-pointed. As you pray, if you shout, "There's a cockroach!" your attention is focused there, not on God. What kind of prayer is that? This is not prayer.

'Umar ibnul-Khattāb ☺, the second caliph following the Prophet ☻, was assassinated while prostrating in prayer. His own groom, the man who looked after his horse, was the assassin. Although the sword had penetrated his body, 'Umar ☺ maintained that prostration until the prayer was complete, he did not feel the sword. He knelt in prostration with the sword in his body. The sword could not be pulled out. He rose and prostrated again, as if unaware of anything else. This was his level of concentration. It was only possible to remove the sword after the second prostration, and it was God's decree that it happened this way. That is the level of concentration we must have in prayer.

This is just a small piece of my own history and my experience. May Allah help us all. *Āmīn.*

April 28, 1974

14 | HOW BAWA MUHAIYADDEEN ﵀ BECAME A BEGGAR

About fifty years ago there was a certain man, a barber, working on a tea estate of about five hundred to a thousand people. The estate collected ten cents a month from each person working there to pay the barber's salary. This man who had a wife and two children was deeply devoted to God. One day he developed typhoid fever. To save him I had to become a barber because he would have been dismissed without pay if he had been unable to work. I had to take his place and do his job for him.

I said to him, "I have come to stay awhile. Since there is no one else to do your job I will do it for you." I treated his typhoid fever, made him well and did his job working as a barber for about three months. In those days hairstyles were different, people wore their hair in a variety of ways, and we had to cut or shave their hair to suit the style. During the three months I did this the "new barber" was greatly respected and liked.

I took care of the clerk, a powerful person on the estate, two days in a row. He came from a *pallan* family which is considered to be an inferior caste. When he asked me where I was from, what my background was, questions like that, I told him, "I learned this trade recently, I am not a barber by birth. I acquired the skill a little while ago, this is my job for now." He did not wear his hair with a knot at the back, it was cut in an unusual style, but I trimmed it nicely in a way that he liked, and he was very happy with the results.

He asked, "Where is the old barber? He did not know how to cut my hair this way. What is he doing now?"

I told him, "The barber is extremely ill with typhoid fever, and I am filling in for him. His salary is so low it is not enough to buy his monthly rations, not enough to support his wife and two children. Because things are so difficult for him, I am working to support us both. We need two salaries now. Since this is the case, could you please try to get him a raise?" The clerk said he would speak to his employer, an Englishman, and try to get the raise. The clerk explained to his superintendent that one salary was being used for two families, and could they increase the contributions of each person by five cents so that he could get fifteen cents from each of them. The Englishman agreed and it was put into effect.

In those days the average salary was thirty cents a day. The barber was now receiving fifteen cents a month from each working person on the estate. He recovered from the fever in two months, and for three months I worked to earn his salary for him, giving him time to recuperate. His pay varied, sometimes as little as seventy, eighty or a hundred rupees a month after expenses, but usually he had a hundred rupees left to support his family. He did have certain expenses, soap, powder, sharpening the razor and so on. At the end of three months I said, "My job is over now, you have an increase of half your salary for your support; you can live happily. The job I came for is finished," and I took my leave. He kept begging me not to leave, and so I said, "Come see me in Kathirakamam next time you go there." He and his wife both wept and cried asking me to stay, but I said goodbye and left. He did come to see me later.

I used to do this frequently, roaming around, doing jobs for people. In one place I worked as a laundryman for someone, in another place I cleaned toilets carrying buckets of waste from latrines. No swami or *'ālim*, no wise man or any of the *'ulamā'*, the learned teachers, could ever imagine the kinds of jobs I have done. I do not know whether any of you could do this type of work either. No matter what was needed, I could fit right in and do it. *Aiyō*, alas, I had so much trouble. If I were to think about compiling a record of all the jobs and all the professions I have had in my life, it would sound like a succession of Purānas, epic tales, so many Purānas. Well, I cannot really call them difficulties. God assigned me these jobs, and I went to do them; that is all.

Even the rockiest of hearts would weep if they heard my story.

Sometimes I worked as a swami. I gave out mantras. I worked as an astrologer and as a temple priest. I have been a poet, a hunter and a beggar. When I was in the Asoka Gardens in Nuwara Eliya there was a man from Talawakelle who was begging for food, and there were two Muslims who also came there having difficulty as well. An Indian whose name was 'Abdul-Rahmān had a large store in Nuwara Eliya which sold dried fish and provisions. I took the two Muslims to that shop and told the shopkeeper to give them some dried fish because they were in such dire need, giving him fifteen cents, a silver ten-cent coin and a silver five-cent coin. "Keep this money," I said, "And give them food." I returned to Nuwara Eliya somewhat later and I realized the shopkeeper had prospered and become rich. Then I brought a stack of betel nut for the two Muslims who were still there to sell, establishing them in this trade. Soon they too became rich. They became suppliers for the big tea estates in the area. Both were devout, praying regularly to Allah, and they thought of me constantly as well.

One day I was coming towards the town when I saw the beggar about to drown himself in the river because he could not find any food, not even gruel. I brought him to the two shopkeepers and put them in charge of him, asking if they would give him some provisions and teach him how to sell these things, how to make a living as a shopkeeper. They hugged and embraced me, falling at my feet. "Please help this man," I told them. The man would put dried fish in a basket which he carried on his head, going around the tea estates to sell the fish, house by house. At the end of the day he would bring the money back and hand the day's earnings over to the shopkeepers. When I returned next time I told the shopkeepers to keep the beggar, who was fluent in Tamil, as their employee in the shop itself, and he became their cashier.

In 1915 there was a civil disturbance which is part of the Ceylonese history of Singhalese and Muslim riots. The Singhalese and Muslims have been deeply antagonistic to each other over the years. During the 1915 incident the two Muslim shopkeepers were driven out of their shop by this beggar, and he subsequently acquired a whole block of shops, all the way from the bridge to the end of the junction. He had killed the older Muslim and his wife, while the younger brother and his wife escaped into the jungle. I saw this from far away, and I came and looked at this in person while I was proceeding to Kandy. From the middle of the war, I decided I had to deal with this.

By then the old beggar had acquired a large share of the business there. He was a big wholesale supplier, very wealthy, and had brought his brother in as a partner. I came down from Jīlānī to the shop where he had first started to work, where he had a quantity of tea, sugar and many things he could have given me. I presented myself there as a beggar and begged, "*Ayyah*, sir, please give me one cent, *ayyah*, please give me a penny." I begged for one cent. He did not recognize me. I arrived early in the morning just as he was unlocking the shop door to open his business. "*Aiyō*, alas, please give me one cent," I begged. Actually, I had started out with five cents in my pocket, but had given two pennies to another beggar on my way, and so I had three cents left. All I asked him for was one cent.

He began to shout at once, "Hey you Muslim devil, you evil beggar, get away from here! Listen you beggar, don't you dare come around here to make me look at your ugly face this early in the morning!"

He used terrible words, filthy words. He had a really dirty mouth. Yet I continued to beg humbly, *"Aiyō,* please give me just one cent." He yelled at me again, and I pleaded, "I have come early, *ayyah,* please give me a little money, just one cent," but he continued to abuse me.

Finally, he went into the shop to get a basin of dirty dishwater from the day before, water the coffee and teacups had been washed in. He took this pan of filthy water yelling, "Get out!" and threw it all over me. The filthy water felt very cold because it was so early in the morning.

I kept pleading, *"Ayyah,* please give me one cent." Water was boiling inside on the stove for tea, and now he took a basin full of boiling water and threw that at me too.

By this time people had gathered around who began to scold the shopkeeper, *"Aiyō,* it's a sin to throw boiling water."

But he was so prejudiced against Muslims he yelled, "You Muslim pig, you dare to come early in the morning to fight with me!"

When the boiling water hit me it felt as if my whole body was burning, but it cooled down and did not blister. Then I said to the man, "I am a new beggar, but you are an old beggar, aren't you, aren't you? You are an old beggar and I am a new beggar. You have forgotten that you are an old beggar. You have only forty days left and yet you have forgotten who you are. I will not go until I receive money from your hand." He was so angry now he kept swearing his filthy words, the least of which were you son of a female dog. He kept shouting abuse at me so furiously I could not get a word in, but I was laughing to myself as I said, "I am a new beggar, you are an old beggar. You have forgotten. Unless you give me a cent I will not leave this place." He raged on.

Soon trucks arrived from Colombo, and the laborers began unloading sacks and sacks of flour, rice and other provisions. There was a Muslim laborer who was unloading some of the sacks. The shopkeeper was getting more and more angry. The laborer came to me and said, "After I unload these sacks I will get my salary, and then I will give you the money."

By now the shopkeeper was picking up coconuts stacked in a corner of his shop and hurling them at me; yet not one of them struck. He must have thrown fifty or a hundred of them at me which I gathered together, piling all the broken coconuts in a heap announcing, "These belong to me now."

This man, angrier and angrier, shouted, "You thief, are you trying to steal my coconuts now?"

I said, "These are mine. All the coconuts inside the shop are yours, but all the coconuts thrown with my name on them belong to me. They do not belong to you because they were thrown in my name."

He picked up an iron bar rushing out to assault me, but he slipped and fell against a drain which lay between us; his leg gave way beneath him as he fell and struck his head on the concrete of the road. The iron bar dropped from his hand. Both his leg and his head were injured, and now all the people watching outside tried to give me money, but I said, *"He* must give me the money." Everyone all around wanted to give me money except this man.

While he was lying on that filthy drain he yelled out, "Even if I die and you die, I will not give you one cent of my money."

The people gathered there humbled themselves before me, begging me to take their money, "Take the money we give you and leave, this man is so angry."

My answer was, "He was a beggar once upon a time; he must know who I am." Then I spoke to him, "You are nothing but a wild man of the jungle who is an ungrateful wretch. When you tried to commit suicide by jumping into the river, I saved you and introduced you to the man who ran this shop. I set you up in business long ago, I established you in this very shop as a cashier, but you killed the owner of the shop and his wife! You beggar of old, have you forgotten? Now you have acquired all these shops and you have forgotten me, you have forgotten me! The exact spot where you tried to commit suicide is waiting for you and your wife. It is calling you. Beware, you have to go there forty days from now."

He was furious and swore terrible oaths. To this day I remember his disgusting words. He swore that way even though his head, his leg, everything, was injured. Then the Muslim laborer who had been unloading the sacks fell at my feet, "This is an insult to all our Muslim people."

I answered, "He is an old beggar who should beware."

The laborer fell at my feet again, "I will give you some money. They owe me ten or fifteen rupees for my work. I will give you every cent of it. Please come with me, this is an insult to all our people, please, don't stay here any longer." He took me to a man who makes *vadai*, a spicy bean savory, and said, "Give him whatever he wants on my credit. I will come back to settle it later with my pay," then he went back to work.

As I sat there another hungry beggar came along who said, *"Aiyō,* I'm so hungry, please give me some food." That evil shopkeeper had also refused to give this beggar any food. Remember, I still had three cents left which I gave the *vadai* seller telling him to give the beggar some food which he took and ate.

Now the *vadai* seller asked me what I wanted, "I don't want anything, I'm just waiting to see an end to that shopkeeper, the one who fell down." When the laborer had finished unloading two or three trucks for which he was paid nine or ten rupees, he came to see me, gave me about ten rupees and bought some provisions which he packed up for me. I told him, "No matter what happens, be patient. Now please leave."

He asked, "Why did you approach that man? Does he know you?"

"That man knew me very well some time ago. He could not have reached this level of success without knowing me. He does not know me now, but in forty days he will know me again."

Then I took my leave and continued on the road uphill. This laborer had two young daughters of marriageable age on an estate called Nānu Ōya where they lived near the railway station in Nuwara Eliya. I went to that estate to give all the provisions the man had packed for me to his two children. I gave them the ten rupees as well, telling them, "Your father asked me to give you this." They asked me to sit down and wait but I said, "I have to go somewhere. Your father told me to give these things to you. Aren't you two married yet, would you like to be married?" They laughed shyly.

On this estate there was a *kangāni*, an overseer, a man who had earned an important position whom I had saved earlier on from a difficult situation. I went to him now to talk about his son, to arrange a marriage between his son and the laborer's daughter. The *kangāni* agreed to the marriage. We found a *lebbe*, an official from the mosque, bought the wedding finery and went back to the laborer's house, who by this time had unloaded two more trucks and was on his way home to the girls. When they saw him they ran to him, "Someone came to give us this bag of provisions and the ten rupees he said you sent."

The man was so surprised he asked, "How did he know I had children, how did he know I lived on this estate? He must be a great saint, see what he has done."

He started to cry, the two girls cried as they ran around the estate searching for me, "We must see the saint, we must see the saint. When will he come again, where did he go?"

Although I had to go altogether about eight miles, I took care of all this in twenty minutes, then came back to the estate with the bridegroom and the *lebbe*, telling the laborer, "I have brought you a bridegroom for your daughter." He fell at my feet and wept. "Here is the bridegroom," I said, "And here is the *lebbe*." Then I provided the *thāli*, the marriage necklace, which they tied around the girl's neck. Because there was another daughter of marriageable age in the house I told him, "You cannot leave this girl alone in the house. Do not go to work tomorrow and I will bring another bridegroom."

Now the bridegroom's father said, "My cousin has a son, a good man, should we arrange their marriage?" I approved, and right then and there we took the girl to this cousin to be married.

"Good," I replied, "Both girls are married, now you can live happily."

The laborer put his hands together, humbly paying his respects, and said, "You have settled my two daughters, I am most grateful."

I said, "I have something else to do and I am leaving now, but I will return in forty days to deal with that other situation." There was a railway bridge on the estate which spanned the river at the point where the road left the estate. On the fortieth day I came to stand on this bridge watching the river. The former beggar came to bathe bringing his wife, a younger brother, the brother's wife and their children, his older brother, the brother's wife and their children, in fact, all his younger brothers and their families. They all followed him, coming to bathe. They left the children on the banks of the river and went into the water, but one child who had been left on the riverbank ran into the river where the current began to pull him under. The shopkeeper rushed to save him and was dragged under, his wife rushed to save the child and was dragged under, the younger brother was dragged under, then the older brother was dragged under, and his wife who also tried to save them was dragged under too. They were all sucked into the middle of the river where there was a steep drop, like a waterfall, they were pulled towards this and drowned. The whole family, including wives and children were all drowned.

As soon as the townspeople heard of the drownings, the other merchants and tailors came running to his shops, looting all the goods. Before the last cry was silenced everything in all the shops was gone. The matter was finished now. The laborer came to me and said, *"Aiyō,* it all happened just as you said it would."

I stood on the main road in front of the shop and shouted, "Hey! That old beggar is gone. The new beggar is here, listen to what he says and seize your opportunity now that it has come!" The dead merchant had persecuted the estate laborers who were very poor. When they used to come to his shop to ask for provisions on credit because they did not have any money, he would refuse. Not only that, he would lift up the women's skirts and kick their backsides. He did so many other nasty, cruel things, he kicked the men as well, and so the estate workers trembled at the very mention of his name. But they had no choice, they had to buy their goods from him. This was the reason this had to be done.

I did not care about his ethnic descent, I cared about his cruelty, especially his disgusting assault on women; he would even go to the estate itself and do these things. If he did give people goods on credit, he would chase after them around the estate trying to force them to give him the money, even though they did not have any. If they did not have it he would beat them and kick them. If the husband was not home he would drag the wife from the house, humiliate and kick her. This was the reason I had to go there.

Now it is finished. All his shops are destroyed and new shops have been built there. This is the reason I had to go as a beggar to that place, I had to beg for one cent. I can still remember the vile words he used to berate me with, I remember the filthy dishwater he poured all over me and the scalding water too. I have not forgotten the coconuts either, how I kept the ones he threw at me which I took to the merchant who sold *vadai,* and gave them to him. The shopkeeper did hurt me a little, I had a small injury on my forehead where a fragment from one of the smashed coconuts had ricocheted off the ground and struck my face.

I begged for just one cent, and because of that one cent all this happened. I just asked for one cent, even though I already had five cents and later three cents in my pocket. "I have three cents, please give me one cent more, my master."

The qualities of that period have left me now. By the time I arrived in Jaffna those qualities were gone. I have been free of them for the last fifteen years.

March 31, 1974

15 | HOW BAWA MUHAIYADDEEN ﴿ﺭﺽ﴾ BECAME A BAKER

I was in the hill country of Sri Lanka to visit a man working on a tea estate who was deathly ill. This man, a great devotee of God, worked in the teashop owned by a European. I cured him and made him well, then as I proceeded on my way I came upon another man who had fallen when he went to take a bath at the waterfall near town. People were standing around watching yet not doing anything, and he was in severe pain.

This man was a baker at a bakery which supplied bread and cakes to the English people who lived there. He had a large business. I thought, "This is a good man," and I lifted him up and asked him where he lived. I found out that he owned the bakery. He had no wife or children, and people were trying to take his money and seize his property.

It was Christmas, business was very good, and although I did not know a thing about baking cakes or about baking anything, I gave him some medicine and said, "Now I will be both a doctor and a baker." Then I took over the bakery.

At that time I did not have much of a beard, I was quite healthy, a vigorous person. When I inquired in detail how they made their baked goods, what they described was not much to my liking, and I looked back to see how they would have done this in former times. Using my inner wisdom, I could see how they made these things long ago, and I found it was better.

There were four huge tables in the room where they kneaded the dough by hand. First they made *gul pāns,* a kind of *roti,* or bun. I do not believe you have ever eaten these; they are not made now. They are quite tasty. I made these buns and the cakes from a very fine grain. The English people who bought these cakes liked them so much they used to give them away as presents. During the four months it took the man to recover, I was the owner of the bakery, doing everything. The actual owner had been in debt for the flour he had bought, but by the time I finished there, the debt for the flour had been settled. Not only that, I had also received as much as seven thousand rupees in presents.

The head of the estate, a European, paid his laborers the equivalent in Ceylon rupees of twenty-five cents a day, while the women earned only twelve cents a day. In 1914 the Great War had begun, and in 1915 there were Singhalese and Muslim riots in Ceylon. This incident must have occurred in 1918 or 1919. At that time the British were in charge of the tea estates, but the laborers were people from Cochin, from Malaysia and some from Java. Those from Malaysia and Java occupied the highest positions on the estates. The Malaysians and the English were the inspectors and on the police force; they were the superintendents of the estates.

I settled about four thousand rupees of debt. I settled all the debts and baked buns, bread and a new biscuit or cookie made from a certain kind of semolina, a larger grain. Today I doubt whether you could find this flour, and who would be bothered to make this cookie even if I told them how? We had a truck the size of a cement truck. A whole truckload of flour, about four hundredweight, which is just under four hundred and fifty pounds, cost one rupee at that time. Flour in those days was only used as paste to glue things together. But I used it to make these cookies and people ate whatever I made. I put ginger essence in some, jasmine and rose in others, some I made with cinnamon. I extracted the essences and used them in the biscuits. They had a wonderful fragrance and people were really fond of them.

In the four months I worked there big crowds came to our shop, thronging there as they did to all the other good stores. We would sell a hundred cookies for fifty cents. The semolina biscuits cost seventy-five cents for a hundred. The *gul pāns* were made of flour, sugar, eggs and turmeric. We would spread this mixture on the table, then keep washing it with eggs until it was ready to be put in a bag which was a kind of mold we baked them in. Each bag cost two-and-a-half cents to make. We made many different kinds of cake, we paid off his loan, and his money box was so overflowing he had to deposit the money in a bank. In those days they had silver rupee coins; his six-foot-long money box was full of these silver coins, it was completely full of bags with coins we stacked there. In fact, although there was very little money in the country at that time, this box was overflowing.

The British would sometimes order as many as seventy cakes, paying up to fifty rupees for each one. They would order a cake, we would send it out and they sent back the money. We did not set a price, they themselves would decide it was worth fifty rupees. They were very pleased with the cakes, and it might have cost us only two-and-a-half rupees to make, including labor and materials. A barrel of eggs cost six rupees, a gallon of milk was eight cents, a rooster or hen cost ten or twelve cents at that time, and you could buy a goat for a dollar fifty. Grape sugar, which we used at that time for the baked goods, cost one rupee for a hundredweight, one hundred and twelve pounds. Both beet sugar and grape sugar cost one rupee, and the flour at that time did not have insects in it. Both the sugar and flour came to the shop in big barrels, ten or twelve a day.

All this went on for four months until the baker was finally better, then he thanked me and I told him, "I'll take my leave now, your debts are paid." Meanwhile, the people who worked there had been given a raise in pay. The owner had been paying them three to seven rupees a month which I raised to twenty rupees, and in spite of the salary increase there was still a huge profit.

December 29, 1976

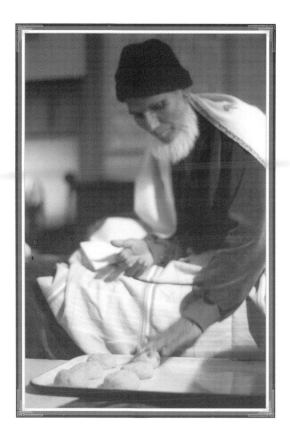

16 | How Bawa Muhaiyaddeen ﷺ Lost His Anger

I n 1955 these words came from God, "Who are you to punish My creations? There is no one on earth without fault, all the creatures on earth have faults. This is the reason I sent the prophets. All those who followed Adam have faults because they are connected to satan. I threw Adam away so that he and those who came after him could be rid of their faults and return to Me in a pure state. They have come to the world to correct their faults.

"I sent you to help them, to correct them, I sent you there to help them overcome their faults. Are you here to help them improve or to destroy them? I sent you to protect them. Are you protecting them or destroying them? Everyone who has come to earth has faults; you were sent down to help rid them of their faults, not to punish them." This is what God said to me.

I replied, "O God, if a man commits an offense once, twice and then three times, I cannot bear it, I become angry. I cannot bear to see this and anger overwhelms me. Take this anger from me. When I see injustice, I cannot help my anger. Please take it from me." I asked this of God in 1955 after a certain incident; then my anger abated, little by little, over a period of twenty or twenty-five years. Before that, could Araby or Gnaniyar have sat here for even a day? Could Dr. Ajwad or Dr. Markar have sat here for any length of time? No, they could not.

In those early days if sick people or someone who was possessed came to see me, they had to sit at a distance. I would take care of their problems in about five minutes just by looking at them, then they would all leave together. They never approached me. They would arrive, I would look at them and they would leave. Now that I have become an *insān*, a human being, you can all be here. Look, everyone sits around me on all sides. It could not have been like this before.

Now I do not say the things I used to say. Since 1956 I have improved a lot, yet once in a while if I cannot bear a situation, the old words will come and if those words come, that is the end of the situation. There is no cure for this. But now I am a good man, a good man with so much love, compassion and mercy. When a child is hurt I cry. I lie down, I cry and ask God to help that child. I am so loving now, I think I am a good man, but I do not know what you think. Now I really am a very good man, and because I am so good it is possible for all of you to be here. In the early days my voice squawked like a screeching bird because I was not used to talking to people. My voice has improved just recently.

My children, no one on earth has performed the miracles Bawa Muhaiyaddeen has. In the last eight hundred years there has not been a single person who has performed as many miracles as Bawa Muhaiyaddeen. This is the truth. Yet I do not understand anything. I am a fool, a fool and a good man. If you become a fool in the world you can become a good man. I give you my love. Go do your prayers and recite *dhikr,* the remembrance of God.

August 13, 1982

17 | ROUNDING

Sometimes you ask me to go rounding, to go for a drive in the car with you, to get fresh air in my lungs and some exercise. I go, but the reasons I go are different from yours. What is the difference? When I go with you to a particular part of town it is to analyze the air in that district. As the air blows over towards me I analyze where it is coming from, what the air is like, what the qualities of the neighborhood, its culture and its people are like. As the air blows past any neighborhood it is filtered through the minds and qualities of the people who live there, and when it reaches me I can identify the essence of the qualities in those minds, what they think, the filth they contain and the characteristics of that neighborhood. I investigate the types of odors, what causes the stench, and by means of this smell I can discover the nature of the area.

You see, if there is a pond used by both animals and people, you can smell it even at a distance. The air above it carries the smell to the areas nearby, conveying the qualities and nature of those who use the pond, sending the stench of fish or the rankness of the animals to places near the pond. Even if the air is pure to begin with, when it passes over the pond it absorbs the impurities there and carries them to pure areas.

Simply blowing across the pond, the air picks up impurities and carries them everywhere close to the pond. People who live there do not have to go all the way to the pond to smell it, because the smell of its qualities and thoughts come to them on the wind.

What you see when you go for a drive and what I see on that drive are quite different. I tell my brother, "Take another road, do not go the old way." I go somewhere else to look at a new neighborhood, its people, its characteristics, and I analyze the smell of the air. From this I understand the condition of people's minds. I understand what they are like, what kind of problems they have, what their problems and struggles are; this is the reason I go for a drive.

When a wind crosses the ocean it carries the ocean smell to the shore.

It brings its coolness, its salty smell and taste, its odor and the smell of its purity or pollution. In the same way, when I go somewhere I can smell the area's purity or its pollution, I can tell what its leaders are like, I can tell the nature of its poverty, its wealth and the tendency for good or bad. From these things I can understand what sort of place it is.

The ocean has many different characteristics, the deep sea, bays, shallow inlets, coves, sandy shoals. There are mud flats where the sea water becomes stagnant, there are pools where the water is clear yet smells foul because of the fish living in it, there are some small rivers running from sea to land, all with a different smell. Although the ocean is huge, it is divided into many smaller areas, each one giving off a different smell. The air is the same air, the ocean is the same ocean, but the smell varies as the wind passes over it: the deep sea smells different from the shore, a bay smells different from mud flats, flowing rivulets smell different from sandy shoals. It is true it is one ocean, but it has many characteristics. The same wind blows, but it brings different smells from different sections; as that wind travels over each part of the sea it picks up the characteristics of the area, its purity and taste changing as it moves.

This is the reason I go to new places, I discover something about the area from its smell. Now we say that we are human, we all need air, we all have the truth as well, but just as the ocean has bays, inlets, mud flats, harbors and rivers, and the wind picks up these smells, human beings also have different characteristics which the wind picks up when it passes over them. There are differences in their actions and knowledge, their qualities and the path they follow. The children of God are all created alike, but just as the ocean is the same ocean with differing areas, the mind of man is divided into various areas. What comes from these different places is what I smell when I go rounding, when I go for a drive.

The smell of the ocean changes in different places. A bay is different, a harbor is different, small pools with oysters and crabs are different, even their names are different. The deep sea smells different from the shallows at the shore, the salt flats smell different from clear pools. In the same way, there is a specific smell coming from the qualities of whatever the mind of a human being associates with, wherever it chooses to stay. My children, I visit all these places to discover this smell. You might also call it rounding, but this is the reason I go rounding. Yours is different. You go to enjoy the view. I go to analyze the nature of the place by smelling the air that comes from there.

Even when I watch television it is different. You watch to see a story,

I watch to analyze how the country functions, to learn something about the qualities human beings have, something about the qualities of the actors. I analyze how this is relevant to the world and whether what they say is true or false. I separate what belongs to truth from what belongs to falsehood, I determine if what they say is true or false. I see what exists in the heart of each person to know if what they portray is correct. I see the reality of the world, I see its act, but you only see the act. That is the difference. You see the road and the people on it, but I examine the smell to understand their hearts, their minds, their actions and their nature. This is what I see when I sit in the car. You call it rounding, but your rounding is very different from mine. Please think about this.

May 6, 1973

18 | THE MEANING OF HIS NAME

Bawa means father, a title given to someone who is the father of wisdom for all mankind. Muhaiyaddeen is a name given to the *Qutb* ☺, the being who brings the divine explanation, who has perfect wisdom. The name Muhammad Raheem Bawa Muhaiyaddeen is a name of light which was given to the *Qutb* ☺, it is just one of his titles. Muhammad means the primal Light which came as a gift from God to all mankind. Raheem is the name of the being who uncovers the primal Light and reveals it. This means that Bawa is the primal father of mankind emanating from the primal Light which is then made manifest. Muhaiyaddeen is the name given by Allah to one who has received the pure Light of God. He is the one who gives the clear light of wisdom, the clarity of *īmān*, of faith, certitude and determination to the heart of man.

That is the meaning of the names which are given only to someone who has the qualities of these names. The names must be appropriate for that person and that person must be a father for all mankind. He must have the capacity to give peace to the hearts of his children, he must guide these children along the right path with the benevolence of the *dīn*, the path of perfect purity, and he must make them understand the difference between *halāl* and *harām*, what is permitted and what is not.

When all the names work together in unity, with perfect qualities, the name Muhammad Raheem Bawa Muhaiyaddeen is appropriate for that person.

July 25, 1983

19 | ACCIDENTS

My child, think about this. According to his destiny a certain person was about to die, and I had to save him for his own sake. He was hurrying to his car to go somewhere when his brother begged me to stop him. "I'll go along in the car," I said, because that was the only way to save him. He would not let anyone else drive his car. Pariyāri, a few other disciples and I got into the car.

We were driving from Jaffna to Colombo, a distance of about two hundred miles. At the town of Chāvakacheri he almost hit something, again at Kodikāman he almost hit something, and then at Kilinochi I convinced him to turn around. On our way back, at Kodikāman once more, he finally did hit something. The car swerved out of control three times, once into a truck, once into a car and we crashed at last.

As I put out my hand to save him I received a terrible blow on my head. The skull bone came loose and my teeth became loose. This happened because I had to save him. No one else was hurt. I told the others in the car to hold my head firmly while I pushed the bone of my skull and my teeth back into place. Before the accident I did have beautiful teeth, and today a fragment of my skull is still missing.

I had to have this accident to save the man, but now there wasn't a car to take me to the hospital. The police wanted to file charges against him. I said, "Never mind, I have to leave," and eventually someone did come to drive me back to Jaffna. My nose was bleeding because of the fractured skull, and we went right back to the ashram where Achi and Rāmeswaram, two devoted disciples, wiped the blood away through the night. The next morning crowds of anxious people came there to find out what had happened, but I said, "Don't worry, nothing happened to me," and I went to the farm at Puliyankulam.

In a separate incident, there was another accident in which I had to save someone else. He came close to death three times and the fourth time he crashed, but I received his injury. Look at my head, there is one furrow here and another one there. The bones in my neck were dislocated, my right arm was broken and my left arm too. While I was unconscious they picked me up and took me somewhere, then to the hospital in Kandy where I knew the doctor in charge. I had put him through medical school. He was very concerned and wanted me to stay on, but I told him, "No, I have to go to Dr. Ajwad's house."

He said, "Then you will have to sign a release saying you want to leave and you are able to leave."

I reached Dr. Ajwad's house that night, but I could not walk because my hip was injured and my nose was still bleeding. The man who had caused the accident drove me there and left. Dr. Ajwad and his wife Ameen, each on one side of the bed, looked after me all night long. What was the treatment for these multiple fractures? Faith in God, that is all. My neck bones are dislocated, my head is still uneven, and although they put makeshift splints on each arm, I still feel pain in the knot where a broken bone healed. Since the time of this accident my strength has decreased, I have had many illnesses and I get pneumonia too.

All this happened to me because I undertook to save someone, but God is the One who saves us. Accidents are possible. The whole world is an accident, everything we see is an accident. Think about right and wrong: the wrong is an accident, and only the right can protect us. Accidents might be caused by our speech or by our food. Our whole life is subject to accident, an accident is possible with every breath. You might not know this, but there is the possibility of an accident with each breath. Please do not feel sad about what has happened to you, my child.

What happened is just one of a million kinds of accidents. Look, I am still alive. If you like, feel my head and you will understand. See how my head is dented as if it were made of plastic. No one else could have survived this kind of accident. My skull was broken, my neck was twisted, no one else would have survived. Even now I cannot walk correctly, I bend and twist to one side.

This does not frighten me, neither should you worry about anything. It is a small thing that is over now. We have more time to reach our Father, and on the day when we do there will be peace. Everyone around us will be sad that we are leaving the world, but we will be happy because we are going to see our Father. Some will feel sad when we leave the world, but there may be some who will say of us, "O he is a terrible man, let him go. It is just as well he left the world."

Others will weep for us and say, "O what a good man, why did he have to leave?" Still, the only thing we need to do while we are here is whatever good we can, and then move on. Please do not be sad, everything will work out well. *As-salāmu 'alaikum,* may the peace of God be with you.

September 24, 1986

20 | THE BOOK AND THE BOX

When I was very young I had a *kitāb,* a book, a huge cloth book about one-third the size of a mattress, the inks for the lettering made of dyes extracted from red, yellow and green leaves of plants. Each page of the book was divided into four sections with a different dye on each. The book was so heavy—it must have weighed between fifty and sixty pounds—and I was so small I had to carry it on my head. The alphabet was hieroglyphic, with symbols of animals like chickens, roosters, horses, lions and tigers, but the book dealt with everything on earth. I had been carrying it around with me for some time when I arrived in the Himalayas where I came across an ascetic sitting there somewhere near the foothills. I traded this huge, heavy book for a smaller one which dealt with heavenly objects, the sun, the moon and the stars, things like that. It was a smaller, lighter book which I took with me.

This second book was written in ancient Tamil, a script not seen much today, which was also interspersed with symbols of the stars, the moon and perhaps some animals. It cannot be easily read or understood, and although the lettering and symbols were intricate, I could bring the characters to life. I could understand their meaning even though I did not know how to read or write. I only had to ask the meaning and it was revealed. If I wanted to know what was written there I could summon a symbol and ask, "Are you the truth, is this the truth written about you or is it a lie?"

This book was the only possession I had except for what my mother had given me, *tasbīh* or prayer beads consisting of one hundred and three light and dark green precious stones with a diamond the size of a thumb worth ten-and-a-half million rupees. There were two other large stones, one on both sides of the necklace, each worth about three hundred thousand rupees at the time, the others worth eighty or ninety thousand rupees apiece. It is difficult to imagine how much they would all be worth now. The large stone, a pure, uncut diamond the size of a thumb, was iridescent. It provided light for me at night, shining with a green radiance. I kept the *tasbīh* in a box.

When I came to Kokuvil, the home of my disciple Pariyāri, I had the book and the box, but there were only seventeen jewels left because I had given the rest away to different poor people so that their daughters could be married. I also kept a supply of *kasthūri*, of fragrant musk, in the box. When I lived in the mountains I had given a tribe of people the rights to look after the deer, and they would collect the *kasthūri*, which has great medicinal value, from these animals and sell it. It was their only income, yet, as an act of devotion, they would always save some of it for me. Whenever I needed *kasthūri* they would be made aware of it, and bring me some. Even though they were in the Himalayas and I was in Ceylon, in Jīlānī, they would know when I needed some. I would come to the town of Balāngoda to meet them, and they would give it to me.

Then in 1942 I gave this box to Pariyāri telling him, "Everything in the box except the *kasthūri* which I need for medicine is for you. It has enough for you and generations of your descendants to live on." But he did not realize its value, and later on when I asked him, "Where is the box that has enough for you and generations of your family to live on?" he could not find the box or its contents. I said to him, "You have lost thousands and thousands and thousands of dollars." This happened in his old house in Kokuvil. Someone must have stolen it. There was a constant flow of people through the house day and night, ten to fifteen thousand used to come to see me regularly. Possibly when we went to get some *kasthūri* the box might have been left open and someone must have seen the brilliance of the stones.

My father and mother had put that necklace around my neck when I was born, and at night it used to give me enough light to travel by. Even climbing a mountain it gave enough light for me to proceed. It gave off a certain kind of luminosity during the day and at night it became a light. When I gave it to Pariyāri I told him he could have everything in the box except the *kasthūri*, but the box vanished. Later in 1949 when I moved from Kokuvil to Kōndāvil, I asked them again where the box was, reminding them it contained everything they and their descendants would ever need, but they were genuine devotees, not interested in wealth, and so they had been careless with it.

All I had left when I went to Kōndāvil was the book I took with me. There are many amazing events from this time, so much that if someone wanted to write my life story it would fill book after book after book with no end to the story. When I left Kōndāvil in 1956 I went to Jaffna, first to a rented house on Second Cross Street for a year, then to another street, Chiviyātheru for six months, and finally to downtown Jaffna.

I kept the book all this time until one day an astrologer asked to borrow it. I said, "All right, take it but bring it back." He took it, and came back soon after to tell me the book had been stolen. If you were to take small sections of that book and publish them as individual books, you would make thousands and thousands of dollars. That man who took it, actually it was the astrologer's younger brother, could not have understood any of it because it was written two or three thousand years ago in different scripts. This theft caused his family many difficulties.

There are many amazing things that happened even in that short space of time, but there is no time now to tell you everything. Perhaps later I will tell you more. Once I start to describe a thing, I have to begin at the beginning and take you to the end, but how can I do this? I do not know how the whole story can be told.

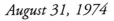

August 31, 1974

21 | A Trip to Kathirakamam

Some people wanted to see the place called Kataragama, also known as Kathirakamam. I asked a disciple of mine named Kandaiya to arrange for a van big enough to hold eighteen people on a trip from Jaffna. I said, "You arrange for the van and I will pay for it." We had to buy huge sacks of provisions because we would need to cook our own meals once we got to Kathirakamam. While I was making these arrangements in Jaffna, Kandaswami, which is another name for the presiding deity of the temple, was telling the priest, the *karpala,* that Bawa was coming. He instructed the priest to make sure we would be received there properly. In Tamil this deity is called Lord Murugan, Kanda or Kandaswami.

It was not the statue that spoke, but the priest was told I was coming. By the time we were setting out from Jaffna, the priest had been told I was coming and he was waiting for us; he had come from the temple out to the path we would take, watching for us.

Just as Kandaiya brought the van he suddenly developed a fever and headache. "Swami," he said to me, "I have a headache and fever, please take the others, but let me stay home." Several other disciples were coming on the trip and someone else was the driver.

I told Kandaiya, "Give me the fever and you get into the van. You have, after all, gone to all this trouble to arrange for the van and deliver it here, you should not miss the trip. Give me the fever and get into the van." And so now I had the fever. From the moment we left, the fever was so high I could not lift my head. When we arrived at Anurādhapura, a hundred and twenty-five miles from Jaffna, the others got out of the van for a cup of tea, but the fever was so high I could not move my head.

From Anurādhapura we went to Puttulam on the east coast where we stopped, about seventy-two miles north of Colombo. By then it was seven-thirty or eight at night, I needed to distribute food to everyone in the van, and I sent Pariyāri and one of the others to find some medicinal oil for my head, but even when I rubbed oil on my head the fever did not go down. I gave out the parcels of food we had brought, everyone ate, packed up what was left and set off once more towards Colombo. From there we continued along the coast to Galle where we arrived at about one o'clock in the morning.

We stopped the car in Galle where there is a rest house. I asked the others to go to the rest house, but I said, "I will stay in the van because I have a fever, I am not feeling well."

They protested, "How can we leave you here with a fever and a headache?"

I replied, "All right, in that case we will give the fever to Shiva." I said to Shiva, "Kandaiya brought this fever from Malla to Jaffna, Bawa Adam brought it all the way from Jaffna to Galle. I have had it for so long I have had enough of it. Now it is time for you to take on the fever and headache. Take charge of this fever and this headache!" Immediately the fever and headache left, and then I was able to take a sip of water, something I could not do before that. I drank some cold water and managed to pick my head up. I told the people who were still protesting, "Look my headache and fever are gone, now you can go to the rest house." One person still insisted on staying with me and I said, "All right, you sleep over there and I will sit here in the front of the van." I sat in the van to do the work I had to do and told them, "Go to sleep, I will honk the horn at four in the morning when you have to get up."

At four o'clock I sounded the horn; they came and we set off along the south coast from Galle to a place called Mātara. There was a devotee of mine named Sandrasegaram Pullai who owned a shop there where we stopped for the others to bathe and refresh themselves with food. Meanwhile, the priest at Kathirakamam had been reminded for the second or third time that I was coming; he kept searching for me, but I was still nowhere to be seen. When we finally arrived at Kathirakamam the priest was standing on the road, outside, waiting for us. He had been given our description and certain signs he could use to identify us.

He approached us, paid his respects and asked, "Is this your name?" I replied it was and he said, "Lord Murugan ordered me to receive you." He showed us around, gave us the history of the temple and behaved very respectfully.

There are small lodges, rest houses around the temple which were all fully occupied, although he somehow had vacated one, prepared it, cleaned it and made it ready for us. Even though the government was trying to improve the water situation, the river near the temple was dry at the time, and so I told Pariyāri and the others to help me dig for water. We placed sticks down and started digging. We dug to a depth of about one-and-a-half feet when water welled up. Then we blocked the hole to keep the earth from falling in, and as much water as we needed flowed. This was the only source of water that day for all the houses in the area and for anyone who needed water.

They all went to the temple to pray, then came back and ate. They knew I had lived near here earlier and wanted to see the places where I used to live. I had told them there were two or three different places where I used to stay. The *karpala*, the priest, would not leave us; he would go and do his work, and when finished come back and stay with us. I told them I used to live at a place called Vallimalai, the name means Valli Mountain, suggesting we could go there, but the *karpala* cautioned us saying that nine people had gone there before and never returned. When he said this everyone was frightened. "Never mind," I said, "Get some flour, some coconuts and water, and let's go. We will take the two dogs stationed at the entrance to the temple with us."

They replied, "The dogs are used to staying at the temple, they will not come with us, they are strays. How can we expect stray dogs to show us the way?"

I said, "If we have to be shown the way they will come. Don't worry, come along," and we proceeded to find the two small female dogs, each about a foot in height. I told one of the disciples who had come with me, "Tell one of the dogs to come with us and be our guide." The dog immediately walked on ahead of us. Everyone laughed, they could not believe it! The dog ran ahead for about a mile on the left side of the road, crossed to the right and came running back, as though she was scouting the land. Then she came up to me and looked straight at me. I told her, "Right, go ahead, keep doing that."

In this jungle everyone is afraid that wild elephants will attack. Someone said, "There's usually a python around here."

But I replied, "Tell it to go and it will." They thought they saw an elephant. I said, "It will go away, if you tell it to go it will go." We could hear the sound of branches being broken by elephants. I told them not to worry, just to keep going. We went on for twenty-six miles until we found a well. It was now almost dawn. We had left in the early morning and had gone twenty-six miles, there were twenty-six miles still to go since the total distance was fifty-two miles. We had told the people at the temple we would return by lunch, to have our meal ready. But everyone was exhausted halfway there as they slumped down to rest. They slept and the dog slept. When I woke them up I told them to bring me the flour, water and some jaggery, a sweet that I mixed into a sugary paste, giving each of them a small ball of this. "Eat it," I said, "We have to go." I gave a little bit to the dog which she refused.

Now everyone complained, "We can't take another step, our legs are dead, we can't move. We are too weak to move ahead or go back. We would rather lie down here and die!"

I merely answered, "Well you are alive now, aren't you? Get up and walk." I put some jaggery in front of the dog again, but she would not eat, she just looked at my face. I said, "Ah, is that what it is, you want me to eat first, do you?" I took a bit of the jaggery, put it in my mouth, then the dog started eating at once. We drank some water, ate the food and I said, "Now we are refreshed, get up, we still have twenty-six miles to go, and then we have to be back by noon." They all said they were so exhausted that they could not move, but I ordered the dog, "Get up, get up!" and I told the others, "The dog and I are going to run, let's see if you can keep up with us." I started running with the dog at my heels, going quite a distance while the others came plodding and panting behind us.

Finally Pariyāri caught up with me and appealed, "Abū, father, please stop awhile, the rest of us will drop dead at this rate, please stop awhile to let us catch up, otherwise we will all die."

I said, "All right, but come, run, run, run. I'm running, my dog is running, why can't you run? That hill over there is not very far away," then the others came panting along. They thought we had arrived at our destination, but I started running again with the dog; we ran and ran and ran. We climbed a mountain. Do you know how long it took us to cover twenty-six miles? Only five minutes. We had walked for six hours to cover the first stage and covered the second twenty-six miles in five minutes. We reached the top of the mountain where we saw something beautiful, a peacock dancing. After we watched this awhile they wanted to bathe in a small pool formed by a rivulet of water coming from a crack in a rock. "Be careful," I told them, "Do not immerse yourself in this water because the pool goes down to the netherworlds. You will never come back if you step in." Then an elephant came to suck some water up into its trunk and bathe. When it went away they all dragged themselves up to the rock and drank and bathed. It was very refreshing because water flowing from rocks is like ice water.

They were relieved and happy, but we had farther to go. Now the footpath leading through the jungle had leopards on one side, bears on the other and elephants might be anywhere. I kept going because we had to climb up farther to reach the cave where I used to live, but two people were lagging behind. This part of the jungle is always full of leopards, bears and elephants. Ordinary people cannot ever come here. They will kill them. I am the only one who could ever stay here. I turned around to yell at the stragglers who shouted, *"Aiyō,* help us, elephants, leopards and bears are going to kill us. We can't move, we can't take another step. We are so exhausted."

I said, "All right," and told the others, "We can't just leave them behind. It is obvious that you are not meant to see this at this time. We cannot leave them. We will turn back." We rested on the rock face on a seat where I used to sit, a seat of rock with two smaller stools on both sides where I would put my feet. We sat there and chewed some betel while we watched a leopard playing with her cubs. I said, "Look how happy they are playing together." Pariyāri playfully threw little pebbles at the cubs. I said, "Now you have had a chance to play with leopard cubs. You have even tossed pebbles at them."

Next I said, "All right, let me show you a secret. There is a cave inside that crevice where you can hear everything happening in Kathirakamam, you can hear the swamis doing *pūjā,* offering prayers and chanting, you can hear the drums." The space inside this rock resembles a cone-shaped amplifier, like the ones on the old gramophones. To get into that small crevice you have to climb down two or three steps. When we did that I said, "All right, put your ear right there and listen. There, can you hear it?"

"Oh yes," they replied, "We can hear everything." It was about nine o'clock. *Pūjās* were being performed at Kathirakamam, they could hear the drumbeat, people chanting and people reciting.

Now it was ten o'clock and time for us to return. I gave them food, again the flour mixed with jaggery, and told them to eat. Then we started off. "I am going to run, let's see if you can run along with me. We have to get there by twelve." The dog and I ran out in front and they ran behind. They had bathed, they had eaten, drunk water and were refreshed. We ran, stopping halfway where they caught up to us. Then I started off at once for the well, the first stopping place, and they ran behind us covering the twenty-six miles in fifteen minutes.

Two of them had been carrying pots of water for everyone. They were so overjoyed with what they experienced one of them balanced a pot of water on his head, dancing in happiness, but the pot fell off and broke. This meant one pot of water was lost and the person who was in charge of the other pot drank it all. There was no water to drink. By the time we got to the well the two stragglers said they could not move another step. Stretching out on the ground they said, "My father, we have walked seventy-five miles, please don't make us go on, just leave us here to die instead, please don't force us to go any farther."

There was one glass of tea left which I shared with everyone, one sip for each of us, then I said, "Right you two, get up," and I spoke to the dog, "Get up and take these two to Kathirakamam. We will follow you." The dog got up, the two of them got up; the dog ran, they ran. The men were stronger now and becoming stronger. About halfway to Kathirakamam one of them lifted the dog to his shoulder, put her on his head and began to run. They reached there by twelve noon, bathed in the water hole at Kathirakamam and lay down to rest. Meanwhile I was bringing the others along who were very thirsty because we had no water. They would walk for awhile, stop and refuse to budge. I promised them some juice from certain jungle fruits, and I found one or two and gave them some. Slowly they got up, Pariyāri first and gradually the others followed. I sent them on ahead, leaving me with Sandaraswami and Clerk. If I walked ahead of them for a mile, I would find them dragging a mile behind me; so I tried making them walk in front of me while I went behind to make sure they would keep walking. We walked and walked and walked, it was very hot and we were walking on stone and sand. It seemed as if it would never end. We had so many blisters on our feet we could not even wear our sandals. By now Pariyāri and the others had already reached Kathirakamam. He came back with water to drink, and the three of us drank some. We felt better and finally reached Kathirakamam at half past twelve.

The dog was still there lying on the ground with everyone else. Once we bathed I told them, "Go and pray in the temple if you want." To the dog I said, "Your duty is over now, go stay where you are supposed to stay. I will call you if I need you." She left and when the man who had carried her on his head went inside the temple to pray, the dog stood at his side. This made him so happy he thought he should give her some food. He intended to bring the dog back with him, but when he arrived he had forgotten her.

Later when I was giving out the food he said, "My father please, the dog gave us so much strength, I must feed her."

I answered, "She will not come with you." He pleaded, asking me to keep some food aside, saying he would bring the dog. He went back to the temple to pray and the dog was at his side again, but somehow he forgot to bring her back. This happened once, twice and a third time. I said, "What are you doing, you have left three times to bring the dog back. Do you intend to share your food with her? Why not give it to the others who are hungry."

He answered, "I don't know what happens, something makes me forget. This time I will definitely bring that dog, I will not forget!"

I told him, "That dog is not a dog who will eat your food, this is not a dog who will eat the food you offer."

"No my father, she will eat it, she will eat it!"

I said, "All right, try." He went to pray at the temple. The dog stood at his side, but he came back forgetting her. I repeated, "This dog will not eat, you will never see her again even if you go in search of her. You had better give your food to the others who are hungry."

Again he insisted, "No my father, please, it may be the fifth time, but I will bring that dog. Let me go." He went back, saw the dog, but when he approached he could no longer find her; he saw her once, but then he could no longer find her and he returned.

Now I explained, "She is not a dog, she is a female deity, the female idol in the temple who is the consort of Lord Murugan. You cannot bring a female deity with you. You can bring a dog along with you, but not a female god. You will never meet this dog again. Don't you realize who she is, can't you see who she is?"

He wept beating his head and chest, "O my father, why didn't you tell me sooner, why didn't I know this before? I have missed such an opportunity."

I said, "Well you did carry her on your head, did you not? We were going to Vallimalai, to Valli Mountain. This was Valli whom I asked to guide us, and she did, but you said she was a dog, and so she came as a dog." He cried and sobbed, weeping with disappointment. "Never mind," I said, "Serve the food to everyone."

There was another pathway leading to a shrine called Sella Kathirakamam close by which we went to see, one of the places I had lived in before. Four of us went, Kandaiya, Clerk, one more and myself, leaving Pariyāri behind to cook. There are two mountains and a river in this place with a comfortable rock seat at about a man's height above the river. We did not take the regular path but a hidden one instead, and we found the rock I used to lie on under a tree, a rock like a bed, it looked like a bed. The surface of this rock is waxy, so soft and smooth, and there is another rock beside it to make a pillow. It was a long time since I had been there. I lay down and felt very happy.

In another place close by there are vines shaped like a swing where I used to sit and swing up and down, but now I lay down on that rock and as the old habits and attitudes came back, I sang a song. When the sound came from me you could hear it coming from everywhere—here, there, there and there, the same music coming from everywhere all around. One man, Kandaiya, seized my foot, another clasped my hand, another held my other hand, all fearing I might vanish because my old thoughts had come back. They heard my song as they held onto me, and I did think of leaving. When I tried to move away I found my foot was held tight, I tried to release one hand, but the other was also held tight. They were sitting around the bed on the ground, holding me, their eyes closed in the sweetness of the music surrounding them, nearly unconscious, dazed and enchanted. Every time I tried to loosen my hand so that I could slip away they would wake up. I tried three times, but they held me so tightly I could not move. Finally my hand and legs were locked in a position that made them numb; I sang for forty-five minutes, but my legs were numb and I had to stop.

I spoke, "Very well, it does not seem to be the right time for me to come, perhaps another time." They could hear me talking to someone, they realized I could see someone. Then I said, "All right, I am not going now, you can let go of my hands and legs. Pariyāri is looking for us, and a wild buffalo is about to attack him along the way. We must go to protect him, release me, we must go back now."

I was sitting on another seat high up, like the one I had sat on before at the rock face, as Pariyāri came along. I could see two buffalo fighting and a third one eyeing Pariyāri, waiting to attack. Waving my hands I yelled, "Stop, stop there!" but he did not hear me, he just kept coming, and so I climbed down the rock. Now you need to know if a buffalo stands motionless, its ears pricked up, this is a sign it is wild, a tame buffalo does not do that. A tame buffalo flaps its ears up and down, but a wild buffalo stands motionless, its ears straight out. This one was standing there watching Pariyāri like that, and then it went straight for him, it was going fast. Its body was fat, about three feet across, but I raised my hand to stop it, and the buffalo was diverted by my raised hand. It went crashing off through the shrubbery.

Then Pariyāri arrived and I said, "You fool, why did you come all this way out here, why couldn't you wait?"

He answered, "We waited and waited, but when we didn't see you I came searching."

I replied, "All right, let us go eat." We returned, served the food, and the next day we climbed another mountain, Kadiramalai, to see the places where I used to live. Part of the area around there was completely dead, yet when I stretched out my hand certain things came to life, flowers and some other things that I picked. When I gave them to the others they were amazed. "Take whatever you want," I said.

This is the story of our trip to Kathirakamam, just a small part, a bit of the story; many other things happened. I did not tell you what happened to the elephants, at any rate, now it is time for dinner. Why didn't I tell you? Well, it did not seem essential to mention everything, let some of it be secret. Even those who saw what happened with their own eyes, those who experienced it are no longer here today. All those who saw these amazing things have changed and gone away.

August 22, 1981

22 | A Vision at the Gates of Hell

I had come to a certain place with one group of people when I saw another group, all crying and weeping. I told those who were crying that I would make sure they would be released, they would not have to enter hell. Then from somewhere else, satan and three or four of his followers appeared. He said, "What right do you have to keep me from taking my people where I am supposed to take them? How can you change their destiny, how can you do that? No one can do that."

I told him, "What you say is quite correct, nevertheless I can change their state. God has given me the right, the license to do this. If I give them this ticket to certify their state, God will change their destiny."

Satan replied, "Well then, try to change me!"

I answered, "You and your followers will never change, not before the world ends or until Judgment Day."

Satan argued, "Well if that is so, if you can't change our destiny, how can you change theirs? This is my destiny, it is also theirs, how can you change one and not the other?"

I said, "There is a specific point here. God has forgiven them and they are ascending to heaven now. All I did was take their hands, I just held their hands. That is the meaning of the license, the ticket. The angels of hell were already holding them, but as soon as I held their hands angels from heaven came down. These seven people had committed sins which doomed them to hell, yet when I held their hands angels descended from heaven announcing that God had commanded them to bring these people to heaven, and they took them up."

Satan repeated, "If you can change their destiny, why can't you change ours?"

"All right," I replied, "Your argument is fair, yet there is a point here, these people were not cursed by God, they are not *mal'ūn*, cursed like you. They committed their sins in ignorance, unaware that they were sins, but you, satan, you knew God, and you knowingly committed sins against

Him. God has given me the power to change the destiny of those who have sinned unwittingly, whenever I intend it and when I think of it. They can reach that station of forgiveness, and if they are already being tortured, God has given me the power to give them the right remedy.

"There is a difference; you are cursed satan, you, your friends and your followers. These people however, were not cursed by God, they only sinned in ignorance, and once they realized what they had done they began to ask for forgiveness. They realized what they had done, and I have the authority to grant them that place of forgiveness. Go away satan, you can never be changed, hell is your destiny. You knew and you acted against God. For that reason this is your state, but they did not know who God is and they sinned in ignorance, they can be pardoned."

Satan retorted, "Well, God has given us this world and hell."

"Yes, that is what God has granted by cursing you!"

Then certain beings went back to their respective heavens while satan and his followers returned to hell. Some of our children were there watching, I cannot remember everyone, but Sonia, Dr. Ganesan's wife Rajes, Ameen and Karin were there. Different men and women were there to be witnesses. This vision occurred at about six or seven o'clock.

April 17, 1979

23 | THE IMPORTANCE OF PRAYER

My children, I want to tell you something about my state and the state of truth itself. I came to the world to do many kinds of prayer, worship and meditation, many kinds of *dhikr, fikr, salāt, salām* and *salawāt*. I am extremely old, both in experience and understanding. I am very, very old.

Long ago there were not many mosques; sometimes you had to walk ten or fifteen miles to find a mosque, you had to walk until *'ishā'*, the evening prayer, then on Friday you had to start right after *'ishā'* the night before to get to *jum'ah*, the midday congregational prayer. I would walk ten or fifteen miles through the jungle, walking all night to reach the mosque about one or two in the morning for the early morning *fajr* prayer. Then I would wait for the *jum'ah* prayer, stay to pray the afternoon *'asr* prayer, the *maghrib* sunset prayer, and walk back through the jungle. I prayed this way without missing a single *waqt*, a single time of prayer, for eighty years.

My state was the state of prayer, my action was nothing but the intention for Allah, my action was the search for Allah, my *īmān*, my absolute faith, was to see only Allah. The purpose of my *hayāt*, my life, was to see Allah and the *Rasūl*, the Prophet of God ⊕. I had no other purpose in life. My intention, my focus and the certitude of my *īmān* were just that.

For eighty years I existed in that determined *īmān*, I sat from one *waqt* to the next, doing *dhikr* and prayer. After every *salawāt*, glorifying God, I did *sajdah*, I prostrated. I have bowed in *ruku'* and prostrated in *sajdah* after one hundred *salawāts*. I did all this sitting in the same place. Reciting my prayers was my state, and what I acquired by doing this, what I realized from this performance of the *salawāts*, from this *husnā*, this inner beauty, was that I received many *wilāyats*, many powers from God. I understood the fairies and the jinns and had many extraordinary abilities.

It was because of this that I also acquired pride and arrogance, displaying a number of worldly abilities. Then I said, "*Yā* Allah, I am searching for You, not for all this."

Then I offered this *du'ā',* this prayer to Allah, "O Rahmān, most merciful One, save me from my state, I am not the one who should control Your creations. You are my God, O Rahmān, please protect me. I did not come here to do this kind of thing. O Rahmān, You are my God, there is no god other than You. You must make Your decisions and pronounce Your judgments, I have not come here to be a judge. You alone have knowledge of Your affairs, You are the ruler and You must investigate this. May You forgive my faults, may You control my anger, may You remove all the abilities given to me. May You end all the tricks and explanations which might come from me. Lead me to the straight, true path. I want You alone, not any other gain. I do not like these powers, these *wilāyats.* O Rahmān, most merciful One, I want Your qualities, Your actions and Your kind of behavior. I do not want any other profit or benefit, I want only You. I do not want to acquire the qualities of this world and its abilities, I do not want any of this, O Rahmān." This is what I asked.

I was like that for fifty years. I would go into caves in the mountains and sit there. I went to many places. For ten or twelve years I sat in one cave on the mountain in Jīlānī. I would sit in different places and pray to Him all during those years, and by doing so I came to know the qualities of Allah's *rahmat,* His grace, and the qualities and beauty of His tolerance. While I prayed to God this way doing all these prayers, I did not miss a single *waqt,* a single time of prayer. Not for one second did I forget Him. My intention did not stray from Him for even a moment.

There are many kinds of prayer and worship in this world which we can do. I have accepted the words of the *Rasūl*ﷺ, and so I pray to my Lord with these words. This is what I need to accumulate for my grave. It is my *hāl,* my state, and I have to say what I have learned, what I have understood about my *Rabb,* my Lord. This is what I have gathered for my grave. My Lord exists everywhere, He is the Lord of the universes, the Lord of grace who is perfect and eternal. I must say what I have learned about His praise and His *rahmat,* His grace. I must talk about this. It is what I earn for my grave. My Lord told me to speak about His praise, His beneficence, about the words of His *Rasūl*ﷺ, and I have to explain, to the limit of my knowledge, what I have learned to those who were born with me.

I have to say this with every breath, I have to say the words of my Lord. This is my prayer and what I earn for my grave. No one should be hurt by the explanations I give about my Lord. I have to talk about it because this is what I have seen. Right now, it is not necessary to tell my children about the grace and love of Allah's *Rasūl*⊕ that I have witnessed. When you are able to understand it I will explain this to you. I cannot explain it right now since it is very difficult to talk about that state of prayer. If you are in the state which communes with Allah and you forget Him for a single *waqt* of prayer, only Allah can judge you. I have not forgotten Him for a single *waqt* of prayer.

My Lord said to me, "Do whatever you do in the right state." Wherever I look I see my *Rabb,* my Lord, wherever I look He is the One I see. I have my *Rasūl,* the messenger of God ⊕, in my heart, and my Rahmān, the merciful One who is my *Rabbil-'ālamīn,* the Lord of the universes, that One with the gracious gaze of mercy who has never left me for even a moment. My task is to pray to Him because I have to answer the questions in my grave.

This is what each of you must earn for yourself. There is no one worthy of worship other than *Allāhu ta'ālā Nāyan,* our exalted Lord who is God. No one else has to explain this to you, no one needs to talk about it or think about it, each person has to do his own work. A person with wisdom wears clothes to protect his modesty, but someone who is insane takes off his clothes because he does not know any better. But a person of wisdom with a sense of honor must wear clothing to safeguard his modesty and honor. Praying to Allah is the thing you have to earn for your own state in the grave. No one else can advise you about this. These are the rules laid down by God. Each of you must do this yourself, be able to answer the questions you will be asked in the grave. If you take this on for someone else, that is satan's undertaking. Each of you must be prepared to answer the questions you will be asked in the grave.

There is no one who is to be worshiped other than Allah. Prayer is an individual experience, a private matter. If you concern yourself with others, that is satan's business. If you backbite you are satan, you are Allah's enemy because you assume His responsibility. If you try to judge someone else you are His enemy. This is my experience, this is what I have to tell you, and it is the truth. May Allah protect you. *Āmīn.*

February 22, 1974

24 | MEETING THE RASŪL ☉

I have seen and spoken with all the prophets since the time of Adam ☉. In 1953 in Ceylon I accepted two Hindus, made them Muslims and gave them new names. They were very loving and did a great deal of duty.

One day I decided to take them to the *Rasūlullāh,* the Prophet of God ☉, to have them accept him and dedicate their lives to him. Once we left the world we came to seven bridges. From each bridge you could see the world. You have to jump higher and higher from bridge to bridge while the bridges shake and vibrate. When you look down you can see the whole world. You can also see whirlpools, quicksand and swamps that suck human beings in. All those who did not understand these bridges were being sucked in and buried in mud.

I had taken these two people with me because I knew something about the bridges which shook so violently. Even when I waited awhile the bridges did not stop shaking as we went higher and higher, until finally we passed the seventh bridge and came to a room with five steps leading up to it. At the entrance to the room there was a person on guard who gave us *salāms,* greetings of peace, and said, "Respected, honored one, have you come?"

I replied, "Yes, I have come to see the *Rasūlullāh* ☉, and I have brought two people to meet him."

The guard told me to come in as he opened the door. Inside I saw a prayer mat and a little platform, but when I entered the room the guard said, "The other two will not come in."

I said to him, "They accept the *Rasūlullāh* ☉, they believe in him, and I have brought them here to meet him."

The guard replied, "O venerable one, they will not see the *Rasūlullāh,* you know that."

And I said, "There are many in the world who have not seen the *Rasūlullāh* ☉, but it is our job to help them do that, we must try. Not everyone is a pure believer." Then I told him this *hadīth,* a true account handed down.

"Our *Rasūl* ⊕ was born in Mecca to Āminah ☺; his father, 'Abdullāh, died before he was born. After his birth the *Rasūl* ⊕ was given to his foster mother, Halimah, who raised him and nursed him with her own milk. Later he went to Medina. Did the people of Mecca or Medina see the *Rasūl* ⊕, did the people of his time ever see him?" They did not. They said the *Rasūl* ⊕ was the child of Āminah ☺, the son of 'Abdullāh, the nephew of Abū Tālib ☺. But who, in fact, was the *Rasūl* ⊕ they saw in Mecca?

"If the *mu'mins,* the true, pure believers, had seen the *Rasūl* ⊕, God would not have created hell, it would have stayed far, far away. We are born as pure believers, yet once we arrive in the world we become *kāfirs,* disbelievers. Our soul recited the *kalimah,* the pure words of faith that wash the heart, in *awwal,* the time of creation. First we said the *kalimah* in the presence of Allah, then in *awwal,* then in the *dunyā,* this world, and finally we must say it in *ākhirah,* the realm of God. We must say it in all four places, we must say it over and over again to become a believer, a *mu'min.* Now we are in this world where everyone is a *kāfir,* a disbeliever, and we have to struggle to become *mu'mins* in a state of Islam, of surrender and purity. Once we become a *mu'min* we will recognize the light of Muhammad ⊕.

"Muhammad ⊕ has many names, many meanings. There is *Āthi Muhammad* ⊕, the manifest, and *Anāthi Muhammad* ⊕, the unmanifest. *Anāthi* was the light within Allah in the time of darkness before creation began, he stayed within Allah. And there is *Allāh Muhammad* ⊕. At the time of creation when Muhammad ⊕ dawned, all the souls dawned as well, and Allah said, '*Yā* Muhammad, without you I would not have created anything.' And with the Arabic letter *mīm,* the 'm' for Muhammad ⊕, Allah did create everything. He created the world as the tiniest dot, like the dot below the Arabic letter *bā'.* We must consider this.

"Those who want to can see the *Rasūl* ⊕ if they are *mu'mins.* The two people I am bringing with me to see the *Rasūl* ⊕ do have *īmān,* I have brought them to the level of *mu'min.* If you can see the *Rasūl* ⊕ you are a *mu'min,* a true believer, if you cannot see him you are a *kāfir,* a disbeliver. Allah is responsible for both, yet we must work hard to become *mu'mins.*

"One day the *Rasūlullāh* ⊕ was sitting mending his shirt at the foot of Mount Hirā' and some Arabs were tending their goats nearby. A tiger appeared and caught one of the goats, but they chased it, snatched the goat back, and the tiger ran up to the top of the mountain, calling out to them, 'Now you Arabs, Allah, the all-Powerful, has given me this food today. You have stolen it, this is not your food, it was meant for me. You have taken the food Allah gave me to satisfy my hunger.'

"One of the men heard this and became very excited, calling to his friends, 'Come quickly, there is a tiger who speaks like a man. It is a miracle, a total wonder!' and his friends came running.

"The tiger continued, 'You are surprised that I speak like a man, you marvel at this, you say it is extraordinary, but what is really amazing is the treasure in Mecca that you say nothing about. You only think it is a miracle that I can talk. The *Rasūl* known as Muhammad, the son of 'Abdullāh born to Āminah, is in the city of Mecca, yet you do not know him. He is the light of Allah, he is the messenger of Allah sent by Allah, he is the mercy and compassion of Allah sent to this world. You do not know the *Rasūl*, you do not know his state which is a much greater miracle than my speaking like a man.' The tiger turned and walked away.

"The men talked excitedly among themselves, 'Who is this son of 'Abdullāh, this child of Āminah, who is this Muhammad? We have to find him,' and they left for Mecca.

"Now the *Rasūl* ☉ was at the side of the road mending his shirt, and the men who came down the road saw him and asked, 'Do you know someone called Muhammad, a *Rasūl* called Muhammad who has come as a prophet?'

"And the *Rasūl* ☉ said, 'O, are you looking for him?' They said they were and told him what had happened with the tiger. The *Rasūl* ☉ said, 'I am Muhammad, the person you are talking about.' Humbly, they asked him to teach them the *kalimah*. He accepted them and taught them these pure words of faith.

"Even in Mecca they did not know who Muhammad ☉ was. Who has really seen him?" I asked the guard.

The guard answered, "I did not say they could not come in, I said they would not be able to see him. Go on in, do as you wish, bring them in if you like." So I went in, telling them to follow me. There was a prayer mat there where I told them to pray, then I went onto a platform below that.

Here I saw the outline of a person covered with a green shawl. The *Rasūl* ☉ was praying on this mat, and I thought, "I must see the *Rasūlullāh*," pulling back the green shawl. There on the mat were nine kinds of precious gems, each casting a brilliant light from *awwal* to *ākhirah*, from the time of creation to the realm of God. I cannot describe this light, a resplendence of indescribable beauty which lit the hereafter. I said, "Yā *Rasūlullāh*, I came to see you. I came to introduce two people who want to meet you, where are you? I see only precious jewels."

He said my name and replied, "I am the jewel in each heart. They call me the jewel Muhammad. There are nine *Muhammads: Āthi Muhammad,* the manifest; *Awwal Muhammad,* the beginning; *Anāthi Muhammad,* the unmanifest; *Hayāt Muhammad,* the soul; *Anna Muhammad,* the nourishment; *Ahamad,* the inner heart; *Muhammad,* the beauty; *Nūr Muhammad,* the light; and *Allāh Muhammad,* the light within Allah. These are the nine *Muhammads,* nine precious gems through which the sounds of the next world can be heard."

I discussed many things with him and I prayed. Then the sound stopped, and the cloth covered the mat again forming the outline of a person once more. I got up and went to look for the two people I had forgotten. The experience was so profound I had forgotten they were supposed to meet the *Rasūl* ⊕. There was no one at the gate, so I locked the door, and then went to look for the guard thinking, "Where is the guard, where is the man who should lock the door?"

Then I saw him. He looked at me saying, "You can lock the door and leave now," but then I saw the guard was really the *Rasūl* ⊕. It was he who had spoken beneath the green shawl, and it was he who was also the guard. I closed the door, humbly gave my *salāms* and left. Who has ever seen Muhammad ⊕? We only say we have seen the son of Āminah ⊕. Who knows who Muhammad ⊕ is, where the sound comes from, what that light, that radiance is? Only when we understand these things will we know.

After this experience the two people I took with me changed. In 1953 they had come to Islam and in 1956 they became disbelievers. First they began to eat prohibited food, they wanted to eat it and they did. It was known they would change, and this is the reason they were not allowed to meet the *Rasūl* ⊕, the reason I was made to forget them when I met the *Rasūl* ⊕. It was only after they left that I realized what had happened and why. From this we can see that *Allāhu ta'ālā Nāyan,* our exalted Lord who is God, knows everything. He knows the heart of everyone, He knows if that heart will change. Even those who are great saints can become disbelievers. Exalted people who have reached high states, who perform miracles, can change and forget Allah. They too can become disbelievers. If one begins to praise himself instead of Allah he will become satan's slave. Only one who is a slave of Allah, only one who surrenders to Allah, will on that day be a *mu'min,* a true and pure believer.

I have seen many things like this, these things do exist. Allah is the only One who knows. He is the *Rahmatul-'ālamīn,* the mercy and compassion of all the universes. He has given us the wealth of three worlds, and if we experience this wealth then we are compelled to dedicate ourselves to Him, to become His slave and to do His duty. When *īmān* or absolute faith develops, then the sound of *illallāhu,* nothing but Allah, resonates within us, and we can attain that *rahmat,* that grace.

Allah is the source and we are His effect. Allah is the origin, the source, the cause of everything, and we are the consequence, the effect of it. He has placed everything within us in one tiny piece of flesh. He has placed His throne, His kingdom, His great wealth, all of everything, in a. tiny room, a small room inside us. Even though it is said to be a room, it is really only a *sukūn,* a tiny circle, a *nuqtah,* a tiny dot in our heart.

No matter how much work we do, no matter what we intend, no matter how hard we try, no matter how much love we have, if we do not think of Allah continually, then nothing will happen. We cannot do anything without thinking of Allah. If we think of Allah we receive everything, if we do not think of Allah He knows we have changed.

I have seen this and been a witness to this. If you think of Him you receive everything, if you do not think of Him you never receive anything no matter how hard you try. I have had many, many experiences I cannot possibly convey to you. His *rahmat,* His grace, is so vast it cannot be described or spoken of.

June 11, 1980

25 | THE QUTB ⊛ ACTS AS A BUFFER TO EVIL

BAWA MUHAIYADDEEN: The day will soon come when I must leave. I am already thirteen years beyond my deadline, and now it is the fourteenth year. Time is passing quickly. After I am gone a war will start. Once I leave here I will also have to play a part in this war.

DR. GANESAN: Will it be the war of destruction in which evil destroys evil?

BAWA MUHAIYADDEEN: There are some who must be saved and some who must be destroyed. Those who belong to God have to be saved; a certain power is needed to save these children, and God told us some time ago this would happen. I have been called to leave so many times, again and again, the last time two or three years ago. On that occasion I had a high fever one night, and all the children stood crying around my bed. When my fever came down I told them what had happened. I had many such experiences at that time. This night I was told, "If you want to stay on you may, but this is a call from God."

My reply was, "I will come, I will return, but please give me a little more time because I would like to correct some of these children and guide them along the right path." There was another call once when I was in Jaffna, and I gave them the same reply then too, "I would like a little more time here." Since then I have not been called, it is about three years since the last call. The good children must all be received by God, while those who are evil are destroyed in the world by the world. What can we do? After that, there will be a time of devastating, terrible hardship, *thambi*, my little brother. If God accepts my children I will leave here. This is what I want. I am waiting for God's word that He will accept and protect my children in the face of any difficulty whatsoever. Once I have that word I will be ready to go. I am just waiting for this assurance.

May God bestow His grace and wisdom on us and protect our children.

I am here with you now, I will not leave right now, however once you manage to reach a certain level, a certain station, I will leave. I will wait until I can take you to a safe height, a safe station, but I am like a broken down hotel van, just managing to drive you along. You can see that this van cannot do much, it does what it has to do whenever it is called, yet the rest of the time it sits around like a broken down vehicle.

DR. GANESAN: You say you are waiting for a word from God. What does God say?

BAWA MUHAIYADDEEN: That war should really have happened in 1960 and again in 1970, however it has been deferred for a little while. God is still calling, He keeps on calling because that serious war should have taken place in 1960. It is still there, waiting; it should have happened by now.

Let us make a comparison. Think of a tree. You can compare a certain tree to the *Qutb* ☺ who brings the divine explanation. There is a certain tree called the *kathpaha virudcham* in Tamil. It is a tree which grants all your desires. The *Qutb* ☺ is also like this. He is a true representative of God. There is only one *Qutb* ☺ in the world at any time.

The tree, with its branches and leaves will trap the winds that blow. It is almost like a mountain, acting as a buffer against the storms and winds blowing across the land. If a gale or cyclone tries to destroy a certain place, as long as this tree exists it breaks the strength of the wind, containing it and reducing its force. As long as this tree exists the forces of nature are contained, its devastation prevented. Only if there is no such tree can the gales and winds affect the place which lies in their path, because when that tree is there this force is contained, with God's permission.

Now suppose I am inside this house with all the children and someone comes to attack the house, to kill the children. Suppose there is property here which belongs to God, and someone wants to throw a bomb at the room. That person will not be able to do it because God's property is here, because the grace, the *rahmat* of God cannot be destroyed without His permission; the bomb cannot affect this room. If someone wants to destroy the people in this room, first, the thing here in God's care must be released from His protection. As long as the grace of God is present in the room, this grace will act to protect everything here from any evil effects. Only if the grace is removed can the storms have their full effect.

This property is the property of God which He protects. Because of that grace, the children who stay behind that grace are also protected.

Therefore, any such evil cannot strike the children with its full force, the grace of God provides a buffer for them.

That is the reason why this body is still here. Notice how the wars which seem to flare up are stopped quickly. This is the reason, because of the buffering action of God's grace. When I was in America last time I could see war flaring up again in Israel because of the oil situation. Oil was the problem. The Americans were discussing the difficulties the oil shortage would cause them, they were discussing the possibility of war. When people asked me about this I told them there would not be a critical shortage, that this issue would not take a serious turn, I told them it would disappear little by little.

Some time later, about a month before I returned from America, I had a vision. I saw myself going to Jerusalem with the *Rasūlullāh* ☺, on our way to al-Baitul-Muqaddas, the Dome of the Rock, before continuing on to the great mosque in Mecca. As we were walking along the noble *Rasūl* ☺ pointed his finger and said, "Look over there." We saw three people coming from the other direction, 'Umar ibnul-Khattāb ☺, 'Alī ☺ and Fātimah ☺.

I asked them, "Why are you here in Jerusalem?"

Their reply was, "Allah has decreed a change of government in Jerusalem. For the time being the three of us will rule Jerusalem. 'Umar ibnul-Khattāb will be the king, 'Alī will be the chief judge and Fātimah *nāyahi,* the noble lady, will be a trustee in the ministry of justice. This is why we have come to Jerusalem."

We joined them and went together to Jerusalem where we established these three in their respective places, 'Umar ☺ as the ruling king, 'Alī ☺ and Fātimah ☺ administering justice. We blessed them and instructed them to conduct this properly, then left Jerusalem for Baghdad and Mecca. At this point I opened my eyes. Did I tell Secretary this when I woke up?

SECRETARY: Yes, I was there. Some others were there too.

BAWA MUHAIYADDEEN: Gnāniyar and Secretary were with me when I woke up, and I told them what I had seen. When they asked me what this experience meant, I told them it meant the war would not gain momentum, that there would be a truce, the oil situation would improve and there was the possibility of peace, and maybe an improvement of the situation in Jerusalem. I told them we had installed a great warrior, a great fighter as the judge to dispense justice, but we made 'Umar ibnul-Khattāb ☺ the king, and he is the embodiment of patience who dispenses justice fairly.

There would be no fighting, no war, the kingdom and its powers had been recast.

Normally 'Alī ☺, a great warrior, would be the right person to be king, but he has been made a judge. 'Umar ibnul-Khattāb ☺, who loves every soul as if it were his own and treats everyone equally, has been made king. During his reign, we have heard that the tiger and the cow could drink water together from the same pond, that the snake and mongoose could live together in the same place, the cat and mouse could live together too. The sword of 'Umar ibnul-Khattāb ☺ reigned at that time, the sword of justice given to him by the *Rasūl nāyaham* ☻. If anyone broke the law, the established code of conduct, this sword would fly directly to that person and cut off his head. It is said that 'Umar himself ☺ never sat on the throne; the sword of justice given to him by the *Rasūl* ☻ sat there and reigned with him.

There is a story about this. It seems that one day during 'Umar's reign ☺, a tiger and a cow, natural antagonists, were drinking water together from the same pond, suspending their usual roles. The tiger drank at the edge of the pond while the cow walked right in, knee deep. Fleas were biting the cow's back as it swished its tail to flick them away, but the tail had been soaking in water, it was wet. Some of the water splashed the tiger who was furious, threatening the cow.

"Do you think you could get away with this if it were not the reign of 'Umar ibnul-Khattāb? According to the laws that normally prevail, you should be running for your life if you see me, but what are you doing? Not only are you walking ahead of me, drinking from the same pond, but you swished your tail, splashing water on me. This is an affront you would never have dared if you were not living at the time of 'Umar ibnul-Khattāb. Otherwise you would be inside my stomach by now!" Before the tiger could finish his words the sword of 'Umar ibnul-Khattāb ☺ had chopped off its head. The sword cut off the tiger's head and returned to the palace.

When 'Umar ibnul-Khattāb ☺ happened to look at the sword, he noticed it was smeared with blood and exclaimed, "This has never happened before in my reign. What does it mean?" And so the sword led him to the cow and the dead tiger where the cow gave evidence of what had happened, explained how the tiger had threatened it and the sword had cut off the tiger's head.

This was the state of 'Umar ibnul-Khattāb's reign ☺, the perfect fairness and just nature of it. I told Secretary and Gnāniyar that this is the person who has now been crowned king of Jerusalem. The warrior 'Alī ☺, the great warrior, has been asked to be judge and Fātimah ☺ is there too. This change happened a month-and-a-half or two ago. This means there will not be another war there now. I told them that there will be an interval of peace, patience will flourish there and whatever happens will not be serious. I told them this when I woke up.

You can see how the war has subsided, although it was actually starting up when I went there, but now it has backed off. If the roles had been reversed, if 'Alī ☺ had been made king and 'Umar ☺ the judge, there would have been terrible wars. This is what I saw. There is a certain power taking care of things in Jerusalem, that power has reached Jerusalem, it is taking effect. This is what I saw when I was in America, then later I saw a few other things, but I could not recall them. This however, I told them immediately, saying as well that the oil crisis would soon ease.

Develop your determination to the state in which your sheikh is firmly entrenched within you. That is all you need, the rest will follow. This is not magic, it is not a mantra. If you slip back one foot the guru retreats six feet. Be steady on the path; if you fall back three feet, he will slip away double the distance. If he is walking ahead of you, follow him. He is the leader. Hold on to him and follow straight behind him. Suppose he walks one way and you turn to look at something in the other direction, by the time you turn back he will be gone. You might see something entertaining and be distracted. You look, then suddenly you remember and turn back to the guru, but he is gone, vanished. He is a light which has gone far away. In the end, you have neither the guru nor what distracted you. Maya has vanished and so has the guru, the light.

The sheikh will not be here forever, he has a destination calling him. If you hold on to him firmly, you might reach the same place he is destined for. The world is a show. There is a lot of show business to look at, but you cannot afford to waste your time looking at that. Instead, you should reach the place where you can see everything, anything you want in all creation, where you can see every secret and every explanation. This is the best, the most wonderful television, it is a mysterious thing with the magnetic attractiveness to pull in the picture, a vision of anything you think of. There is no such instrument in all of science; the instruments of science can only take you so far, take you to a certain place at a certain time, and these instruments must be in the right place at the right time to capture the picture on film. But this television can take in the whole of *awwal, dunyā* and *ākhirah,* the time of creation, this world and the realm of God, the world of *dēvas,* heavenly beings, the world of the soul and the world of illusion. All of these can be seen at one time. This is the magnet of all magnets with an unbelievable capacity. God has created such an instrument.

My children, if you want to reach God you need to learn the truth, you need the truth. You came here to learn this truth so that you can reach God. This truth is the guru, and there should be no doubt or difference of opinion about that point. What he says is right, whatever he says is right: be very determined about the truth of that point. If you develop a different idea about it, you have lost the point.

A tree may ripen with thousands of fruit attracting as many as fifty thousand parrots who come to sit there from time to time. Each bird takes some of the fruit and flies away. In the same way, the guru produces millions and millions of fruit which ripen during different seasons. Fruit ripens at the appropriate season, crops developing continually through the different seasons, different times of the year and different decades. If you are like the parrot and merely listen to three or four words, and if the moment your stomach is full you fly away, you will never be completely satisfied. When the tree is laden with fruit you take some and fly away, but when it produces no fruit you run away, not waiting for the next crop. This is an ever-bearing tree. Although it is seasonal it does continue to bear at different times. Just because there is a change of season, you who are man pick up what you want as your circumstances dictate. When there is fruit you take it, but when there is none you leave.

If you merge with the tree, just as fertilizer becomes part of a tree, you will be fully absorbed by it. Or if you wind yourself around the tree like a vine, the essence of the tree will flow into you. The tree's qualities, its sap, its taste and essence will pass into you if you wind yourself firmly around it. But if you are like a parrot, merely pecking at one or two things that you hear, you will leave. A vine that winds around a huge tree never dies. Any kind of tree entwined with a sandalwood tree also emits the fragrance of sandalwood. Mere proximity allows it to give off the fragrance of sandalwood. In the same way, you should wind around the sheikh. This is faith.

Let all the qualities of the tree seep into the vine. Receive its food, its water, its fragrance, everything. As long as the giant tree lives the vine also lives, taking its nourishment from the tree. If the tree is cut down you are cut down with the tree. If the tree withers and dies you also wither and die. If the tree goes to heaven you go to heaven too. This is that state of faith in the guru. Then you will not die.

When you pick up words or instruction from here and there, you resemble a parrot who flies to the tree in one season, eats a piece of fruit or two, then flies away. This tree bears a certain kind of fruit in one season, another the next season and a different one the following season. The taste is different, the fruit is different in each season. If the parrot flies away thinking the fruit is all gone, it misses the next season of fruit. It should have waited for time and circumstance to make the tree bear the right kind of fruit.

This is an explanation of the relations between the sheikh and a disciple. All the vine has to do is wrap itself firmly around the tree without asking questions. Asking questions is not its function. Asking why the branches point north or why a leaf grows a certain way is not the business of the vine.

My children, may Allah protect you all.

March 26, 1973

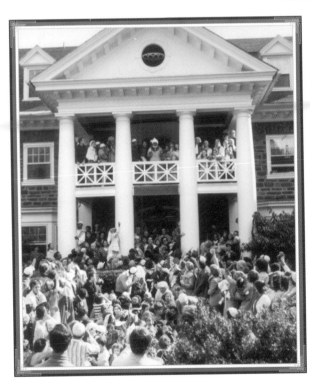

M. R. Bawa Muhaiyaddeen ☙ (on porch, center) and Fellowship members at the central branch of The Bawa Muhaiyaddeen Fellowship located in Philadelphia, Pennsylvania, circa 1978.

26 | A JOURNEY FROM MEDINA TO BAGHDAD: HOW TO RECOGNIZE THE TRUTH

Certain people here have been following the path of their mind, following the mind but thinking it is God leading them. They announce God says this, God says that, as though they were hearing God speak directly to them. This is madness. How can God speak, how can He appear, how does this happen? What is that vibration and how can you receive it? What is the point here? The mind presents a television show, a magic show called maya or illusion. This is the ignorance, the darkness which makes people insane. If you engage this state of ignorance you will experience hell. For some time certain individuals have been doing this, and it is wrong.

A true vibration does not come that way because true vibration is wisdom. How do you receive this vibration? You have been saying vibration, vibration, but the vibration is wisdom, a mirror you will see. Which world are you looking at? Do you see where God lives, can you see it, can you actually see where God lives? Do you really think you see where God is? You certainly cannot; so how can you call this thing a vibration? Describe the sound, how does it come?

If you are lead by this idea without understanding it, if you follow the path of the mind, it will lead you into great danger. You are merely doing whatever your mind tells you to do. If the mind says bring me some meat, you eat meat, if the mind says do not eat meat, you do not eat meat. If the mind tells you do not go there, you say God told me not to go there, and you do not go. What is the point of this? If the mind tells you to give away your wealth, you give it away. If the mind says take off your clothes, will you take off your clothes? If it says to pull out your eye, will you do that? If it tells you to give up your other eye, will you do that too? A man came yesterday who had a directive to go out into the snow, to take off his clothes, and he did that. Your mind might tell you to go to the jungle and live there. Are you going to do that?

This is incorrect. This is not the way. You have to study wisdom and learn the difference between right and wrong. There is a right and wrong. The mind says bring me a chicken and you bring it a chicken. Does God tell you to do this, does God send this vibration? You must reach a state of wisdom, a state of *gnānam*. Do not take the route of madness and ignorance! If you keep saying God says this, God says that, this is insane. It is the monkey mind telling you this, it is the influence of maya. It sounds just like the man who wanted to go to heaven, but was persuaded to have a look at hell first.

First understand wisdom. Wisdom is a light which is the resplendence you must acquire from your sheikh. By using the mirror of wisdom, see the difference between right and wrong. Then you will see God, you will see yourself, you will see everything. That actually is light, but if your mind tells you God says this or God says that, it is only the antics of your monkey mind which has its origin in the five elements. These are the antics of the mind, of satan, ignorance and darkness. Throw such thoughts away, catch that monkey and tie it up at once. The moment these ideas come, immediately recite the *subhānallāhi kalimah,* the third kalimah which is a purifying prayer. Say, "Go away satan," and blow into your chest. They will go away. Say, "Burn satan, burn," and they will burn up.

Please listen to a story which is part of my history. When the Prophet Muhammad ⊕ went on *mi'rāj,* his mystical ascent, everything all along the way spoke to him: cows, goats, grass and weeds, everything bowed in homage, speaking to him because he had a certain fragrance. God said, "My fragrance exists within whoever has the truth of God. The prophets, *nabīs,* and the lights of God all have My fragrance. My Light is present in them." And this is the reason that animals, snakes, demons and ghosts all bow down in homage the moment they catch that fragrant scent.

Once when I was traveling from Medina to Baghdad I knew of a shortcut unknown to the others, and decided to take it over the mountains, a very rocky, treacherous trail. Two of us traveled together through the cliffs where there were many rattlesnakes, cobras and other poisonous snakes hiding among the rocks. The moment they saw us the snakes slid over to us, spread their hoods, bent down and gave us *salāms* saying, *"As-salāmu 'alaikum,* may the peace of God be with you."

The man who was traveling with me exclaimed, "These snakes are talking! Why do they bow down before you? Poisonous snakes bow in homage to you, why do they do that?"

I answered, "Ask them, ask them that question."

And he did ask one snake which opened its mouth and said, *"Allāhu ta'ālā Nāyan,* our exalted Lord who is God, informs us of the birth of each prophet and great one. Reptiles, demons, ghosts, jinns, fairies, birds, heavenly beings all are informed when a prophet or a great being is born. Allah informs us, 'I have caused the birth of this prophet, I have caused this fragrance, this beauty, a being with these qualities to be born, I have made My Light appear. I have created all the prophets, the lights of God, the *qutbs* and *gnānis,* beings of light and wisdom, and that is the reason My beauty and My fragrance manifest in them.' Whenever one of these beings is born, this announcement and a command are sent by Allah. This fragrance will be known to all living creatures. Because we saw the light of the *qutbiyyat,* the divine explanation, because that fragrance, that beauty and light come from you, as God has ordered we had to bow down in homage to you. This is the reason we lowered our heads and said *as-salāmu 'alaikum.* We did that because the fragrance was evident."

This is what the snake told my companion as it bowed in reverence. "Is that the way it is?" asked the man. The cobras bowed again and left us while we kept going. Then my companion said, "That snake spoke like a human being, how did it do that?"

I answered, "God has said, 'Using the triple Qur'an, the *thiru marai* of *Allāhu ta'ālā Nāyan,* our exalted Lord who is God, I have created *insān* or true man.' Within *insān* lies this *thiru marai.* The moment a man becomes *insān,* a true human being, and reaches the station of *qutbiyyat,* which is the divine explanation, then that Qur'an in his heart becomes who he is. He becomes that. Since that *qalb,* the inner heart, is the Qur'an itself, every letter that is in the Qur'an is being guarded by angels, jinns, fairies and heavenly beings. These beings are guarding and protecting this Qur'an, this heart. Each and every letter in the 6,666 verses of the Qur'an is being guarded. The *qalb,* the inner heart of such a one, is the Qur'an.

While the jinns, fairies and heavenly beings guard this heart they are also traveling with the *qutbiyyat,* they are there with the *qutbiyyat.* There is a guardian for every letter of the heart, and those guardians come too. It is the heart which is the Qur'an and these heavenly beings are the guardians of it.

"When you came with me you thought I was taking you across a dangerous mountain with piercing stones, snakes, thorns and no water. You thought, 'If I go with him I do not know how we will reach our destination.' It is what you were thinking, were you not? That is the reason this was shown to you. Who is the One who provides water for these snakes, who feeds them, how do they live here, who gives them food? This happened to explain all that to you. The snakes who spoke were really jinns and fairies protecting the Qur'an within me. They did that to demonstrate this power for you. That is the reason they spoke. Understand that the jinns and fairies showed you this because of the doubt in your mind. That is the reason they demonstrated this."

The man confirmed, "Yes, that is exactly what I had been thinking."

We traveled farther and came upon some people drinking water, "You said there was no water in this rocky place, did you not? But look, they are drinking water, let us go closer." As we came closer the people disappeared, the people disappeared but the water and the cups made of rock from which they had been drinking were still there. I said, "Drink some water. You thought there was no water around here, but look, there is water. Drink some." And so he drank some water and I did too, scooping it up with my hand. It tasted sweet, like the juice of a coconut, like sherbet. It was delicious. I asked him, "Do you see how sweet it is, how delicious it is? There is no sugar in it, but it is sweet."

This was what happened on the journey from Medina to Baghdad. Since certain beings are protected in this way, if you say God talks to you or vibrations come to you from God, people will think you are insane, and this is not the truth. You must acquire God's truth and that good wisdom which is true. This vibration of truth cannot be explained. When God wants to be revealed, His beauty, His fragrance and light appear. The moment they appear, everything lies open for you. Everyone, without prompting, bows down in homage to you. This is the way it is, not as you describe it.

The way you talk is the way the false swamis, the business people and false gurus talk. The truth is not like this at all. Wisdom is not like this, light is not like this. If the truth, wisdom and light manifest within you, they will be identified immediately. All those who look at you will be dazzled, they will tremble. As soon as they see these, the fragrance is obvious. But even ghosts, jinns and heavenly beings fly away when they look at the state you are in now. If you keep saying that God is talking to you, this is hopeless. Anyone who knows the truth will say you are mad, they will say you are out of your mind. Please use your wisdom to reflect on this.

June 2, 1975

27 | PROPHETS AND QUTBS

QUESTION: What is the difference between a *Qutb* and a prophet, what are your duties? We have a sense that you do a lot more than the things we see.

BAWA MUHAIYADDEEN: My brother, the prophets came to repeat the commandments God gave them. God instructed each of them, "Go, tell this to the people," and each one came and repeated what he was told to say. The prophet received the sound, the message from God, and as a microphone relayed it to everyone. When the sound first came from God it came as a secret, then it was transmitted through the microphone so that it could be heard everywhere. This is the mysterious way God's secrets were revealed and made available to mankind.

The prophets could not say whatever they wanted to say, they were limited to repeating exactly what God commanded. Some prophets had more power than others, and for that reason the commandments they received varied in strength and number with the state, the actions and the capacity of each one. In the same way that a child is given instructions appropriate for its age as it develops from stage to stage, the sound and commandments given by God varied from place to place, from time to time, according to the capacity of the prophet and the needs of his people. This means that from the very beginning, as wisdom grew, the strength of God's commandments also grew.

The duty of a *Qutb* ☺ differs from the duty of a prophet. Prophets revealed secret commandments given to them by God, something like a salve you apply externally for pain, but the *Qutb* ☺ goes within, as a secret within a secret. As people change, the *Qutb* ☺ notes the change and then gives whatever injection is needed for the particular disease. As wisdom within wisdom, the *Qutb* ☺ goes within and gives the necessary explanation.

The sounds of the prophets reach only the first three levels of consciousness, feeling, awareness and intellect. These three levels can be explained by an example. When an ant crawls on our skin first we sense an itch through feeling, then awareness tells us where it is and intellect urges us to scratch it. The words of the prophets come first to feeling, then feeling conveys the words to awareness while awareness brings each message to intellect. The commandments of the prophets come to us outwardly, teaching us through feeling, awareness and intellect; we receive them through intellect and follow them. The *Qutb* ☺, however, is different. The *Qutb* ☺ goes within, beyond intellect to deeper levels, and as we grow this wisdom shows us, point by point, the meaning at each step. First as subtle wisdom, then as divine analytic wisdom, the *Qutb* ☺ keeps identifying and analyzing each point, explaining everything to us. This is the difference between a prophet and a *Qutb* ☺.

The prophets bring sounds to feeling, awareness and intellect, but beyond these levels you have the judgment or assessment needed to evaluate your life. The *Qutb* ☺ functions as higher levels of wisdom, first as subtle wisdom which helps you understand the subtlety of each point, then the *Qutb* ☺ becomes divine analytic wisdom which explains what this is, what that is, analyzing the difference between them. Finally, the *Qutb* ☺ becomes the *Nūr*, divine luminous wisdom, the completion which tells you this is His power. The state and the function of the *Qutb* ☺ is the wisdom which works within.

June 16, 1979

28 | THE ANT MAN QUTB☉

God has not sent an ant man like me to the world before. I am the only ant man for this world and this *yuga,* this time period. After my time, it will be difficult to find a true guru. Destruction will prevail, wars will prevail, magic will prevail. My contract is coming to an end after all these years. In fact, my agreement was actually over fourteen years ago. One word, only one word from God gave me this chance to stay fourteen more years.

According to all my earlier predictions, everything that I said would happen is happening now. What I predicted before was that as the destruction of the world approaches, magic will increase, mantras will proliferate, false gurus will appear and the religions will become businesses. Thieves, drunkards and murderers will become gurus, women filled with lust will become gurus. Scoundrels will proclaim themselves to be god, using magic and tricks to receive important titles. Faith in God will change, modesty and decent conduct between men and women will change, the four attributes of modesty, reserve, sincerity and fear of wrongdoing will change. Lust will increase, abortions and stillbirths will increase making menstrual disorders multiply, creating new kinds of disease. Terrible sickness, cancers, tumors and viruses will be rampant because of this failure in morality.

I also said that in the coming time gurus will develop many potent evil forces that deny God and generate sinful, satanic qualities. I said justice will wane, envy, jealousy and vengeance will increase, everything will become some kind of business, something selfish. A man with six or seven children will cast off his wife, find another and start a new family; a mother with six or seven children will leave her husband, her children, and find another husband. Races and societies will change. A time will come when sons will sleep with their mothers and marry them, daughters and fathers will have sex with each other, brothers and sisters will have sex and marry. This terrible conduct will occur, the forces of satan and illusion will make progress, people will fly in the sky.

These statements were told to me and made by me one thousand years ago. I said this would happen. I said people will fly in the sky, they will report that God does not exist, and this will cause deadly wars, wars of atoms, of bombs. Faith in God will be lost and the destruction of the world will come to pass. There will be famines, devastating rains will fall, deadly fires and increasing warmth will eat up the world and this will increase disease. The taste of food and fruit will change, harvests will diminish, disease will be spread through food, water and the consumption of prohibited food. People will forget God. These are the things that happen at the time of destruction. I was told I would see these signs before I leave the world, and I can see this happening now. It all started before the end of my agreement fourteen years ago.

I have been called back three times, and three times I asked them to be patient. I actually died and came back to life each time because some of my children cried and cried, begging me to stay, to take care of them. When I came back the third time I asked for a special favor, "There are a few children I need to teach awhile; keep me here for that much time. I ask this favor." The children were all around my bed as I asked for this, Dr. Ajwad on one side, the others sitting at the foot of the bed, everyone crying. The angels were also all around my bed, but I had to say, "A few of my children are with me here, I have to guide them a little while longer. O God, the time of destruction has come, give me a little more time to protect my children. I will teach Your truth to everyone and then come back to You."

I could see the angels assembled in the heavens which were decorated with indescribable beauty, with flowers and ornaments. There were great crowds waiting for me there, but I told them, "The time of destruction in the world is approaching, and there is still a little more for me to do. I must go to the west because I have made my intention to go there, and I have even made preparations for the trip. I must go there to take care of certain things. It is important for me to go to the west and offer certain explanations. Please give me permission to do this."

They replied, "We are suffering here too, waiting for your explanations. Please understand we have been expecting you, and God has commanded us to open up the heavens. Look, see how beautiful it is." The angels cried and wept and the children here also cried and wept, Dr. Ajwad, his wife Ameen, his sister Gnāniyar and a few others.

I answered, "It is essential that I travel to the west to proclaim this truth."

They said, "We need the truth too, we have been suffering since you left."

Then the sound of God came, "Very well, whatever you intend, let that happen. You may do as you wish." With those words I opened my eyes and told a few people what had happened. That was just a few days before I came to America for the first time. I had been deathly ill for eighteen days, then on the eighteenth day I opened my eyes and told them this. Once I had said it, I was better, I got up immediately, went to Jaffna to arrange everything there and four days later came to America.

These are the words of God I am revealing to you now, something of immense value, yet I am only telling you a small part of it. What happened was God's will. I am a very tiny ant man in this world, but in this *yuga,* this time period, you will never find another guru anywhere like this. If you have found a true guru, he is the right guru for this time, this age. After his time, if you should want a guru, his children will have to acquire that state, and it is through these children that the destruction of the world might be reduced or delayed to a certain extent, because this is what is coming now, the destruction of the world. This is the way it is.

Do not think that what I have brought is something easy. Analyze it with wisdom and try to understand. This is the truth, it is the truth. This is the word of God. If you understand, you will realize this. At whatever level your intellect and wisdom are, accept what you can.

There is only one *Qutb,* one embodiment of the divine explanation, at any time, and the *Qutb* who is here now has outlived his contract by fourteen years. There is only one guru, one *Qutb* for each *yuga.* He is the *Qutb* for the time of the three major prophets, Moses ☺, Jesus ☺ and Muhammad ☺. Use your wisdom. This is your chance. If you miss it the opportunity will disappear and it will be very difficult to have this again. You will fall prey to a maya guru, a mantra guru, a karma guru, a *matham* guru of fanaticism, a magic guru, so many other false gurus, sixteen different kinds of false gurus.

May God protect you. *Āmīn.*

January 8, 1974

29 | The Mosque

About fifteen years ago in Ceylon in the middle of the 1960s, during my meditation I saw that the whole world was in darkness, a darkness within which some quoted from their religion, howling, shouting and leaping around. I wondered, thinking to myself, "These children remain here without light on the outside or within. They make all these peculiar noises and jump around in this state of darkness." Then I raised my hands to God, "O God, these people are in a state of darkness, they live this way. O God, what does it mean?"

At that moment I saw the *Rasūl,* the messenger of God ⓢ, who was with Dr. Ajwad, Ajwad's sister Gnāniyar and myself. There was another lady off in the distance who might have been Fātimah ⓡ. We were trying to establish the mosque I was building. We dug beneath it to lay electrical wires enclosed in pipes so that the entire mosque could be lit from top to bottom. If you gave the *adhān,* the call to prayer, from that mosque the sound would be heard all through the eighteen thousand universes, and the light from this mosque would radiate through the eighteen thousand universes as well. We built the walls of the mosque to a height of about twenty-eight inches.

While we were working I noticed a group of people farther away on a hill, a mountain, who were shouting and calling for Dr. Ajwad. What were they shouting about? They were actually abusing and reviling me, speaking ill of me, calling Dr. Ajwad to come over to them. At this point the *Rasūlullāh* ⓢ and I were standing together there, and I laughed. The *Rasūl* ⓢ called me by name and said, "Are you laughing?"

I replied, "When all praise or blame belongs to Allah alone, *yā Rasūl,* O Prophet of God, what else can I do but smile and laugh if people speak this way?" When I said this I looked towards those people and told Ajwad, "They are calling you," but he was angry because they were insulting me. I said, "They are calling you, you had better go to them."

Then I saw that the mountain was on fire with an indescribable intensity which was consuming that group of some five hundred people. Since Ajwad had now left me to join these people, Gnāniyar began to shout, "Bawangal, Bawangal, great one, please save my brother, he will be burned by this fire." She was wailing and crying as she rushed over to me. I replied, "That fire will never touch those who have *īmān*, those who have absolute faith, don't be afraid." When I looked again I saw that all the people there except Ajwad had been burned, but another woman who was pouring out abuse and threatening me came rushing towards me. The *Rasūl* ⊕ and I were standing together there as she came to attack me, holding some kind of weapon to assault me with. Some distance away from where we stood there was a grave which she fell into as she ran.

Once she had fallen in, the *Rasūl* ⊕ and I went over there to look, and we saw the grave was filled with snakes, worms, reptiles and insects which were eating this woman, biting her, stinging her. I cannot describe the way she howled and shrieked with these snakes and insects stinging her again and again. I cannot describe her anguished cries and lamentations. I said, *"Yā Rasūl,* see the state this woman has come to." The things biting her were things she had searched for in her life, things that came from her mouth and her heart. The worms, the snakes and centipedes were things she had held in her mouth and her heart, and now they were biting and stinging her. She had brought them with her; this was what attacked her now.

When we returned to the site of the mosque we were building Ajwad had also returned, and I told him, "I expect there will be poverty, famine and every difficulty in this country. We must establish a cooperative store to provide food or other necessities for these people. We must do this. You will have to be the manager who will take responsibility for feeding the people." I put him in charge of this shop which I stocked with everything he would need. But certain people came to cause great conflict there, they tried to destroy this cooperative store, they tried to destroy it completely. And so I said, "We will complete this mosque someday. It will take more time, but it will be very beautiful." When I finished my meditation I opened my eyes and told Ajwad, his sister and some others who were there what I had seen. This was fifteen years ago.

All this did happen. The people there did go through so much hardship, and whenever they got into trouble the very people who had been reviling me came to ask for my help. All that had to happen was occurring in stages. What is the meaning of the cooperative store that was established for poor people? It means that every day sometimes fifty, a hundred or a hundred and fifty people who had to be fed three times a day came to see me. This was the cooperative store they tried to ruin, creating every kind of problem in their attempt to destroy it. Many people tried to ruin this organization, yet no matter how much they tried, the Fellowship, this house and this child Ajwad are still here.

A little later I saw a celebration in my meditation, I saw a kind of fortress extending up to the fifteenth sphere, rising up to the highest point in the sky. I was the head of it, its leader. I had to tell a *hadīth*, the traditional accounts, make the speeches and give the explanations. I am telling you what really happened. There were many steps in each sphere. You had to climb gradually to the fifteenth sphere, a total of fifteen spheres to climb. I had been invited to this celebration and I had to attend. On the first floor, where it was announced that everyone should assemble, there were two guards. One of the guards was the angel Mīkā'īl ☺ and the other was another angel. As the people arrived there, they would show them where to go, but some were turned back.

When I reached the first floor they took me over to the stairs and told me to climb up while the two of them remained there. There were about twenty-five people who accompanied me, Ajwad, his wife, Gnāniyar, Araby, Dr. Markar, Husain and his wife, Hilmy Muhaiyaddeen and his sister, certain others, about twenty-five people altogether. Although many came, many were also turned back by the two angels.

Once we had reached the top certain other beings, angels and heavenly beings joined us. When I looked down from the top I saw that other people had joined us, not only the people who had come with us from the first floor, but some who came from other directions. There was a stage there where I had to sit to discourse, where I had to make a speech about Allah and the *Rasūl* ☺, about these different spheres and their stations. I also had to speak about life and death.

I cannot really describe everything we had there, all kinds of unimaginable fruit, grapes and other amazing delicacies. As I was concluding my talk they brought me trays filled with this fruit, fruit unlike anything you will find here in this world. Honey oozed from them, it dripped from them as I shared them with all my children. "Come, take this, these are the fruits of heaven. Come, take this, taste this heavenly fruit," I offered.

There were two people in the group who had been refused admission on the first step, but I had told the two angels to make room for them, to let them come, and they were here. When I realized they did not come up to receive any fruit, I noticed this and said, "I will not offer you fruit from my hand again. If you do not want to taste it from my hand, at least taste it from someone else who has this fruit, take something to eat from that person." And they both left while the others ate. After we finished eating I spoke, "This is heaven, you have now tasted the fruits of heaven. I appeal to God to let you visit here again, but you must also intend to come. You must intend to leave the world and come here to unite in this fifteenth sphere. You have tasted this fruit and you must live in this heaven." This is what I asked of God, then it was over. I opened my eyes and told those who were here about it. This happened some fifteen years ago.

After that we came to America in 1971, eight years ago, then when we came back to America again in 1973, in my meditation I saw myself building a mosque here in America like the one I had started in Ceylon. You could hear the *adhān* all the way to *ākhirah*, from this world to the realm of God. This was the kind of mosque I was building, the angels, the messengers and myself all coming together to build this mosque. We constructed the mosque and the dome, and all that remained to be done was painting the dome. Everything else was finished. Its beauty, its light were indescribably beautiful, light radiating everywhere. It was the most beautiful mosque. Only the last coat of paint for the dome had to be put on. Again, I told this to the children who were here.

There is a mosque in *firdaus,* or heaven. The mosque built by me here in America is like the one in heaven. It is possible to find people in America with the kind of *īmān,* the kind of absolute faith you need to reach that *firdaus.* There was just a little work left for this mosque to be complete, and once I did that I told the children, "The mosque I could not complete in Ceylon I have completed here in America."

August 24, 1979

"God's House" in Mankumban, Sri Lanka, designed by M. R. Bawa Muhaiyaddeen ☜, built by Fellowship members and dedicated February 17, 1975.

The Mosque of Shaikh M. R. Bawa Muhaiyaddeen ☜ in Philadelphia, Pennsylvania, designed by M. R. Bawa Muhaiyaddeen ☜, built by Fellowship members and dedicated May 27, 1984.

30 | THE DISCIPLE MUST MERGE WITH THE GURU

My children, there are nearly one hundred members of this Fellowship who have accepted the guru. Only when you take refuge in the guru will you receive grace. You must unite your heart with the guru's heart and hand your responsibilities over to him. Let them be his. Hand over your body, your possessions and your soul to the guru. Your body must become the guru's body, your life itself should be the guru himself—your body continues as the guru's body while the life within you is the guru. Give every responsibility to the guru who lives within your body. This is your soul, your life. When you surrender all responsibility for everything this way, you will discover how to reach that state of merging and living within the guru.

During the last eight months nearly eighty thousand people have come to this Fellowship, but only a hundred stayed to take refuge in the guru; the rest who have many other teachers or gurus come here to pick up something from this market, but what they pick up is only an echo, it is useless. What you learn without a teacher has no top or bottom. Only when you surrender all responsibility to the teacher does the knowledge of a disciple have a living current, otherwise it is like an echo, it bounces away. Many children have taken teachings from here that way. The sound they take from here bounces off, it does not penetrate; they are like a car with no driver. Many children have picked up these teachings this way and left. They take the teachings here, analyze them with their own wisdom according to their own teacher and abilities, and then they try to extract a certain grace from them, except they cannot find that grace. Only the true teacher who offered the teaching understands its explanation. You cannot use your senses, the elements or what you see to analyze the meaning and grace of this teaching. What you learn without a true teacher does not stay with you anywhere.

If you wish to reach God you need a teacher, a true *gnāna guru*, a *Qutb* with the qualities of God; you will find all the attributes of God in this

173

teacher. When you take refuge in such a guru you will see God. You become the guru, disappearing in him while the guru disappears in God. Three flames become one God. God is a flame, the guru is a flame, the disciple is a flame. As the two disappear in One, this is the triple flame. Children, please understand this extraordinary process.

Your guru, your teacher, is not here just for you. You do have a teacher who will take you safely to a good place, but he is not an ordinary guru, an ordinary teacher, he is a very precious teacher. He might be here for a little more time in this world, however when he leaves, if more children come through your effort, please teach them what I have taught you. My children, you must accept the children who come, make the guru responsible for them and act appropriately. This is what I ask of you.

It may be that the guru you have is very good, it may be that the teacher you have is the only true teacher in the world. You may not be able to see that teacher now, but once you surrender all responsibility to him, when you look you will understand who that teacher is. To see the guru who is not looking for any profit from you, who is only carrying out God's commands, you need firm faith and certitude. He will not spend his time expecting to receive your food, your favors or what you have gathered. He is neither worldly nor learned, and therefore my children, every word that comes from him is a sound coming from somewhere and someone else. From time to time he will speak spontaneously using these sounds, but he will not say anything without God's permission and His command.

There will always be four or five witnesses when he transmits these words. This is the way it is, this is a secret. Your guru is a secret, you are a secret, God is a secret and the world is a secret. You must have the supporting faith, certitude and determination necessary to know these five secrets. Do not think you alone have the right to escape. Others will come to join you and your guru. With love, hospitality, God's compassionate qualities, with all the appropriateness of patience, tolerance and peace, and with the three thousand gracious qualities of good thoughts, you must show them love and your good qualities. Guide them on the good, true path to God as you are being taken now. If they come asking to join your Fellowship, if they ask you to find them a guru, you must do this to help them. You must take them in.

The whole world is a wonder, it is magical, and magic always causes fatigue. When people are acting and dancing they are happy, but once all that is over they are exhausted; only when they are tired do they understand the advantage or disadvantage of bodily exhaustion. When they are exhausted they need treatment, they feel old and tired, they feel that death is approaching. Then they will come running to you, tired and worn saying, "O God save me. Show me God, where is God?" This is the way they will come searching. When they arrive in this condition take them in, connect them to you and take them with you on the good, true path. Embrace them as brothers and sisters and teach them what you have learned. Give them what your guru gave you.

My children, each of you must persevere and be diligent in guiding them to this good path. This is what I ask of the hundred children. It is very good to accept those who come in the future. It is very good to take them to this good path. If they come here to attain the good station you have reached and to attain the good, true path that you have attained, then please accept them. Please take them in.

The divine wisdom imparted through the words of the guru—what is taught according to the words of the guru—is exalted divine wisdom. You must have faith, certitude and determination in the guru's teachings. The true wisdom of the guru, the true words of the guru and his true blessings are the true powerful forces within the mystery of this path of truth. Only when the disciple is accepted by the guru will he be accepted by God.

No matter how much you may learn any other way, that knowledge is like a pumpkin or a melon drawn on paper. If you pick up things here and there, this kind of learning is like a pumpkin illustrated in a book, it cannot be used to make food, it cannot be eaten or cooked in a curry. When children who have not received the teachings, offerings and the grace of the guru pick up things from here and then leave, the things they take are just like a melon or a pumpkin drawn on paper. What they pick up here will not help them when they are in danger, they cannot eat it or use it. It is like rain that falls into the sea, you cannot drink it because it becomes salty sea water. If the rain falls in places where it should fall, if it stays in the places where it should stay it will not be salty, it will be drinkable. Then it can be distributed through the pipes of a water system as good water. The teachings of the true teacher only quench the thirst of those who have fallen into him. Otherwise that teaching will not quench the thirst.

There is just one prayer, one meditation through which one can see God. The one who worships God must be God Himself. The one who does God's duty must be God Himself. God must pray to God, God must see God. If the worshiper is separate from God he will not see Him. The disciple must emerge as a child from within the guru. The faith, certitude and determination in the heart of a disciple must be buried in the guru and take form there. This absolute faith must fall into the guru, become an embryo in the guru, grow within him and become the form of the guru. Then when this child emerges he will be in the form of the guru. When this child emerges he will be in the form of light. He will not have the physical body, he will have a body of light. This is the formless state. This is God, this is the form that will see God. Unless this happens you cannot see God. If you think you can have this once the guru dies, you will find it difficult. While the guru is still here you must learn, become an embryo and be born.

A teacher who drinks alcohol is not a true teacher, a teacher who uses drugs, marijuana for example, or who drinks beer, brandy and whisky is not a true teacher. You must drink only God. Feast on His qualities. If we try to list all the abilities and qualities of the guru, it is like trying to count the grains of sand in a sandpit. If you could count the grains of sand in a pit one-and-a-half feet deep and one-and-a-half feet in diameter, you might find out something about the quantity the guru has to offer, or his age, or the secrets or commands of God that exist within him. If you try to find out something about such a guru with your monkey mind, your desire and what you see, if you try to figure out what he contains, it is like trying to measure the ocean's water with a little measuring cup. He will look at the measuring cup you bring, laugh and say it is all right. He will assess what you have, what you are like and laugh to himself.

If you want to clean the dirt from yourself, first fall into the pond, and in the same way, only if you fall into the guru and surrender to him will you know his depth, breath, coolness, taste and joy. Just as you find comfort by falling into a pond of water, fall into the guru who carries out the commands of God, see what is there, disappear within him. Since you will be a living embryo inside him, you can run around and see that city, you can know the secrets of the guru, you can see the eighteen thousand universes, God, yourself, your life, your teacher and everything within him. You can find clarity.

When you bring your cameras here to take a photograph of the sheikh, you never catch his real image, you only take pictures of the forest hiding his secrets. His real secret is never revealed to you, you see only what can be photographed, but you do not see the secret within that. My children should think about this. I have told you this so that you can learn how to worship and how to meditate on God. Please think about this, understand it and act accordingly.

April 26, 1972

31 | A Prayer for His Children

My children, if someone asks you to teach them the truth, then definitely teach what you have learned. But do not ever fight or argue. For God there are no fights or arguments. For Him everything is love, everything is in the form of love, compassion and truth. May God grant you the blessing and grace to live in that state, to live in that form of compassion and love, to live together as brothers in unity.

Because of my children's love, because of God's love and His command, because of that divine assignment, that divine request, I came here from Ceylon to this country. I have given birth to you children, through the love of God's qualities, through His love and the love of the heart. I gave birth to you with His compassionate love, my children of compassionate love. I gave birth to you through the interaction of His divine love and compassion, through the bonds of love, wisdom and the love of the heart. Uniting with His love and compassion, I conceived you in that love. I raised and nurtured you within that wisdom as His children, and I have given you over to Him saying, "O my Father, here are Your children born through Your love and wisdom, conceived in love where we joined in love. They have emerged from wisdom and have been nurtured in wisdom." I delivered you to Him saying, "Here are the children born to You and to me in Your wisdom and love, please accept them. Look at their beauty and Your beauty, see Your beauty in their beauty. Please accept these children born to You."

I showed Him your faces and your hearts in that form of love, and I gave you to Him, saying, "These are Your children. You and I joined together, conceived them and brought them forth. They emerged as lights of wisdom and received Your beauty in the light of that wisdom. They are Your children whom I have given birth to with Your beauty. Please look at these children I conceived, accept them and give them Your qualities and the wisdom that is suitable to them. They are now Your responsibility." I said this, and I testify that you are His children, and that I have handed over all responsibility for your development to Him.

A thousand years ago there was another opportunity like this when certain children were born who developed to a very high state. Since then, even though I spent many years in Ceylon, only a few children have been conceived in this state. Now, in the time that I have been here in America, a number of children have been conceived, and although they are still infants, they have been given form, they are growing and are completely His responsibility, His charge.

Earlier, when I was younger, I was able to look after the children I conceived, to help them grow and develop. Now the time has changed and these children are like children born to an old woman. Because they are born to an old woman, because it is the era of the end of this world, the time of this world's transformation, I have placed them completely in His divine charge and given God the responsibility for their sustenance and development. I said, "Their growth and development are Your responsibility. This is the period of destruction, the changing of this world. Please look after them."

Many years have passed for me. I am old now and the world is also old. Many transformations, changes and forms of destruction will occur in the world. At this time, because of the aging of this world and because of my age, I have received so many children at the same time. I place them all completely in His divine responsibility.

My loving children, my children who were created with God's beauty, my wise children, whatever difficulty you may have, do not ever leave His charge. Just as the prophets of God kept their faith firm and were tolerant in spite of the problems they had, no matter what difficulties you may experience, be tolerant, be forbearant and embrace all living things as your own life. The truth will never leave you, and the Mother and Father who gave birth to you will not leave you. They will remain, staying in your love and wisdom. The moment you intend this, you will be able to see it within your body, within your eye, within your heart, within your love and within your wisdom. If you look into the form of love, if you look into the form of wisdom, you will see your Father. He will not leave you. In a state which is neither dream nor thought, it will be possible to see Him. You should never be upset or sad about this. You should never waver from the truth.

> Hastiness is the enemy of wisdom,
> Impatience kills wisdom,

> Anger is the guru of sin,
> Lust is greater than the ocean,
> Duty is greater than God.

Service to God, your truth and your wisdom are His duty. Do not forsake that duty. All that glitters is not gold; do not to be deceived by those glitters. God's truth and His wisdom are true gold, they are true wealth. The wealth of wisdom has no limit, this limitless wealth is His grace. The treasure of grace receives whatever needs to be received, and this is eternal. A golden pot needs no decoration. The beauty of God and His divine grace need no decoration because they are His beauty. If you fail to understand this, it will be like the action of one who does not deliberate carefully and has to suffer the pain of a living death.

Where were we before, and what section does this belong to? What is this connection, this part of the body? What are the things connected to this body? Who and what is within this 'I' and what belongs to God? What dies and what does not die? What is within this body, what leaves, what remains and what is put into the earth? What goes to heaven, what goes to darkness and what goes to light? What goes to death and what goes to birth? What has an end and what is endless? What has a shadow and what is without shadow? Who are we, who is God? These are questions which must be understood, analyzed, known, investigated, seen, identified and sorted out. This life, this body, the human appearance, the human form, human life, physical sense, physical spirits, God's wisdom, His grace and His light must be distinguished and understood. If all this is not understood, life will be filled with sadness and distress. It will be a life of dying without dying. Understand this.

You must understand this and receive the beauty and the splendor of knowing who you are. May God, the protector and sustainer, provide this beauty to all of you. May He provide wisdom, completion and grace for all of you, and may He embrace you within this beauty and love. The ocean of patience is still, it never moves, while the ocean of illusion is in constant turbulence. The ocean of illusion which is the mind is never still, it is constantly turbulent. It has to be thrown onto the shore of forbearance. When the waves reach the shore of forbearance they are turned back. In the same way, you must build this shore, board the ship of patience and use the rudder of wisdom to steer the ship. With the anchor of grace holding the ship, load it with His divine love. Bestow goodness and His compassion on all living things, then disembark on the shore of His grace.

There you will see the brilliant, radiant city of His Light, an endlessly brilliant, radiant Light. Our Father, the omnipresent One, exists in the radiance of that brilliance.

You should not miss this ship. You should climb into this beautiful ship. Whenever you are in distress or have a problem, whenever you are in any kind of difficulty, never give up your steadfastness and determination. As the year has four seasons, as the wind blows in four directions, as there are four worlds, many different things rise up in a person. There is sun and there is rain, there is ice and snow; this is the *dunyā,* the world. The four seasons and the winds change; the four religions are also like this. They are different seasons. There are four different seasons, and they will come. This a season, that is a season.

It is not false. When there is snow there are no birds, then when it rains the birds return, the plants grow and the trees produce leaves. During the hot summer you have to leave for a cooler place. This is the way the seasons come, and among God's creatures there is also a change of seasons. The winds blow, seasons change, but He alone exists without change of season or climate. He is Truth and He has no seasons. He exists forever, always, as Himself. Everything else changes. Man is born, man grows, man becomes old and man dies. These are his four seasons, which change. But God was never born, He was never young, He never became old and He never died. Truth, wisdom, the soul and God do not have four seasons, they are not born, they do not grow and do not die. May God bless my children and have them reach that path of truth.

I have roamed through many countries for many years, but this is not the moment to tell my history, to tell my story. Now that I have given birth to these children it is not the right time to reveal my story. The book is there, the story is there. If you want to know who your Mother and Father are, it is there in that book. When you can understand, when you reach an exalted state, look at that book and receive your kingdom. Everything is written in that book, all the details are written down there: this is for so and so, that is for so and so, this is for so and so, this piece of land belongs to so and so. When you acquire wisdom, when you have that maturity and look, you will take possession of the deed. Take it, read it, find out what is yours and take that for yourself. The deed given to you has now been printed on the children's treasure chest of the heart. It is there in that box. When you acquire knowledge, open the box and read what is inside. You will know the secret. When you know the secret you will realize the history by yourself, you can write it and see it for yourself.

There are certain things that can be told and certain things that cannot. There is a secret. What I have put inside the heart is there already in that book. When you have maturity, when you look at that deed, the connection will be clear. I gave you something for your heart in the same place that the book is kept. When you are mature, when you have enough wisdom to look at it, you will see the connection, you will understand what you need to know and be able to write what you need to write. But just now, in this or any other country, it is not possible to give an account of my history. The book is kept there, in the heart, and you have to read that. When you have wisdom and maturity, and when you look at it, you will see your story, you will see everything. Then you can identify your own share and take that. Then those children with intelligence will be able to read it. May God grant you wisdom and the eyes to read the deed He has given you.

This is what I have to say to my children. What else is there for me to say? All I can talk about is your love. Children cannot understand their mother's love, it is not possible to talk about a father and mother's love, but we can talk about the child's love. Parents can talk about their children's love, and it is your love, the love of your hearts that I describe, that I talk about when I travel to other countries or other states. It is not remarkable for me to describe a mother and father's love, but your love must be praised.

I have to leave in about six or seven days, and once I go I should be able to come back again. There is your love, my children's love, yet it is God's duty, His will, whether or not I return. But there is something that does not come and go which will not leave you, which will always be with you. That thing which has neither coming nor going has taken life within you and is alive there. In the form of wisdom, in the form of grace, in the form of love, this thing is living within you my children, and it will not leave. It is under divine protection, under the protection of God Himself. It will live with you and protect you. Only the part which is the body, the senses, this part which is the physical body needs to go to Ceylon to do certain things, to provide certain kinds of comfort. Once this is done I can return.

My children should accept the qualities of God. My dear children, whatever mistakes certain children might make, it is up to you to protect yourself from fights, quarrels and disagreements. We are all children of one mother, and even if mistakes are made, if fights and quarrels start, you must try to tolerate this, try to be patient and forbearant, try to live peacefully in unity. Never let go of the qualities or the forbearance of God.

Love all living things as you love yourself and accept all beings as your own. Please live this way.

I implore each of you to adopt these qualities. Never let go of your patience, never let go of your compassion or forbearance, accept every child and live peacefully with each other in unity. Mistakes will be made wittingly and unwittingly. In such situations, it is better to adopt patience and tolerance, accept these children and show them the right path. This is the best thing to do. May God grant you these qualities, this wisdom and plenitude. May He grant you the perfection of love, the excellence of wisdom, the flawlessness of grace, His perfect wealth and the perfection of light. May He have your hearts live in the form of love and the form of His divine radiance.

O my God, may You live in the heart of each and every child, may You protect and sustain them. O my God, grant us the grace of being light within our heart. May You be light and sound always shining, pulsing and resonating in the heart. O my God, fill the bodies of my children with divine grace, make them shine with gold, make them with the imperishable metal of Your grace. O my God, protect them from the waters of illusion contaminating their blood, their muscles, their skin and their flesh, protect them from sickness and disease, protect them from the satan of arrogance. Protect and safeguard them with the light of Your grace, destroy all sickness and disease. Let them exist in the form of light, protect and sustain them.

O my God, please let their eyes shine, let their sight always be there, let the light of their eyes penetrate everything, see everything and shine upon everything. May You protect them. Please grant us this. O my God, with Your grace let their ears always hear Your sweet sounds, Your sweet voice, Your sweet resonance. Let their hearts be joyful upon hearing Your sound and Your explanations. Let them be joyful when they see Your light. May honey trickle from their hearts upon hearing that sound. O our Lord, grant them the grace to have You live on their tongues as their speech and words, displaying Your love, Your compassion and light. Live on their tongues, always emerging in the form of Your stories and discourses of wisdom.

O Rahmān, most merciful One, every material thing, all the wealth, the body and the *rūh*, the soul, are in Your hand, Your responsibility. As You safeguard our wealth, our bodies and lives by day and by night, whether sleeping or waking, through happiness and unhappiness, please safeguard my children, protect and sustain them. Please grant us this grace.

It is Your concern, Your responsibility forever. Now, in the hereafter, the past, the present and the future, may You alone be their protector, their friend and guide. May You protect, sustain and help them, O God. In sleep and in wakefulness, may You alone sustain and protect them.

Āmīn, āmīn, yā Rabbal-ʿālamīn, O Lord of the universes.

May 31, 1972

32 | ONLY GOD HAS A HISTORY

INTERVIEWER: Could you please tell us something about your personal history for a short article?

BAWA MUHAIYADDEEN: My child, the history of a human being cannot be written. Understand that the human body is formed by the twenty-eight letters of the Arabic alphabet which make up the true Qur'an, the inner Qur'an. Since man's anatomy has been composed of these letters, how can it be written down as history? In fact, man's body is the Qur'an which contains the entire universe, the grace and plenitude of God. Can you ever hope to describe this, to write about this? God Himself is the One who writes. There is no dictionary, there is no language and there are no words which can describe Him. God's history is what we must understand.

Man is merely a student who has come to this earth to learn the history of his Father. He is just a little child with no history of his own. If you want to write your personal history you have to start with the place where the body was formed, and that is hell. This body of earth, fire, water, air and ether begins its story there in the seven hells from which there is no escape.

You have to go back before this beginning to the story written by God, to the history of His grace because there can be no other history but God's. If you write only His history with no story of your own, there is no judgment for you, no world, no heaven or hell for you. When the 'I' no longer exists there is no history, no beginning and no end. There is only God's history, one history whose explanation is truth. The explanation of this truth is divine wisdom, the explanation of divine wisdom is the resplendence, the explanation of this resplendence is overpowering, omnipresent light.

Can you put this history into words? Since His history has neither beginning nor end, it will never end and will never be destroyed. Understand where you were before. When did you come here, why did you come here, how would you describe the history of the One who sent you here? To know the answer to these questions is to know the truth and history of the connection between God and man. My child, this is what you must learn.

July 13, 1973

Some forty miles from Philadelphia, among the rolling hills and tall trees of Chester County, is the *Mazār*, the resting place of Muhammad Raheem Bawa Muhaiyaddeen ☙, who passed in 1986.

QUESTION: You have told us before that your body is very old. What will happen when it dies?

M. R. BAWA MUHAIYADDEEN : What has to die will die, and what has to remain will remain. Supposing you dig a well and the water dries up. Just because the well went dry, you cannot say that there is no water there. You cannot say that the spring is dead, for if you dig down one more foot, water will again spring up. If people will only dig a little deeper, they will find the water there. Of course, they can say, "There is no water in the well any more," and go away. But those who have real thirst will dig a little deeper, and they will find the water there. What is will always be. That which dies is dead and gone, but that which is will always be.

December 8, 1978

GLOSSARY

The following traditional supplications in Arabic calligraphy are used throughout the text:

⊕ following the Prophet Muhammad or *Rasūlullāh* stands for *sallallāhu 'alaihi wa sallam,* may the blessings and peace of Allah be upon him.

⊕ following the name of a prophet or an angel stands for *'alaihis-salām,* peace be upon him.

⊕ following the name of a companion of the Prophet Muhammad, a saint, or *khalīfah* stands for *radiyallāhu 'anhu* or *'anhā,* may Allah be pleased with him or her.

(A) Indicates an Arabic word

(T) Indicates a Tamil word

(S) Indicates a Sanskrit word

(U) Indicates an Urdu word

abū (A) Father.

adhān (A) The call to prayer in Islam.

ahādīth (A) (sing. *hadīth*) In Islam, authenticated accounts relating the deeds and utterances of the Prophet ⊕. If the words or commands of Allah were received directly by the Prophet Muhammad ⊕, it is known as a *hadīth qudsī.* Words of wisdom; discourse of wisdom. *Ahādīth* is sometimes used to refer to the traditional accounts of other prophets as well.

Ahamad (A & T) The light of the beauty of Allah's essence *(dhāt),* which is the inner heart, called the *aham,* or *qalb;* the sixth of the nine Muhammads ⊕.

aiyō (T) An exclamation, alas, O no!

ākhirah (A) The realm of God; the hereafter; the next world; the divine world.

al-hamdu lillāh (A) All praise belongs to God. All praise for everything that has appeared and everything that comes to an end is due to God alone. When you say, *"Al-hamdu lillāh,"* you praise Him saying, "Everything is Yours."

alif (A) The first letter of the Arabic alphabet (|). To the transformed man of wisdom it represents God, Allah. There is a beginning and an end, but Allah alone is eternal, existing forever naturally as the natural reality. For Him there is no beginning, end or destruction. He alone is Allah, *alif.* Then and now He alone exists.

ālim (A) (pl. *'ulamā'*) Learned one.

Allah or *Allāhu* (A) God; the One and Only; the One of infinite grace and incomparable love; the One who gives of His undiminishing wealth of grace; the One who is beyond comparison or example; the Eternal, Effulgent One; the One of overpowering effulgence.

Allāh Muhammad ⊕ (A) The light of Allah within Muhammad ⊕ and the light of Muhammad ⊕ within Allah; the ninth of the nine Muhammads ⊕.

Allāhu ta'ālā Nāyan (A & T) God is the Lord above all. *Allāhu* (A) Almighty God; *ta'ālā* (A) the One who exists in all lives in a state of humility and exaltedness; *Nāyan* (T) the Ruler who protects and sustains.

ambiyā' (A) (sing. *nabī*) Prophets; messengers.

āmīn (A) So be it. May God make this complete; may it be so.

Anāthi Muhammad ⊕ (T & A) The unmanifest; the name given in *anāthi,* the beginningless beginning, to the *Nūr,* God's resplendent light; the first of the nine Muhammads ⊕.

Āndavan (T) God.

Anna Muhammad ⊕ (T & A) The food and nourishment for each life, the fifth of the nine Muhammads ⊕.

arwāh (A) (sing. *rūh*) The invisible divine realm; the station where Allah resides; the world of pure souls. Lit. souls; light rays of God.

'asr (A) The afternoon prayer; the third of the five daily prayers in Islam.

as-salāmu 'alaikum (A) "May the peace and blessings of Allah be upon you." This is a greeting of love. *As-salāmu 'alaikum, wa 'alaikumus-salām.* One heart embraces the other with love and greets it with respect and honor. Both hearts are one. In reply, *wa 'alaikumus-salām* means, "May the peace and blessings of Allah be upon you also."

Āthi Muhammad ☉ (T & A) The manifested; *Āthi* is the primal beginning, when the essence *(dhāt)* of Allah emerges from Him; the second of the nine Muhammads ☉.

a'ūdhu billāhi minash-shaitānir-rajīm (A) I seek refuge in Allah from the evils of the accursed satan. "Please annihilate satan from within me and burn him up. *Minal* (T) is the fire of the resplendent light that comes like lightning. In the same way that lightning strikes, burn him away from me. Burn satan who is the enemy to the children of Adam ☉. He is the one who has separated us from You, O God. Please prevent that enemy from coming and mingling within us. Prevent him from coming once again into our midst, and take us back to You."

awwal (A) The time of the creation of forms; the stage at which the soul became surrounded by form and each creation took shape; the stage at which the souls of the six kinds of lives (earth life, fire life, water life, air life, ether life and light life) were placed in their respective forms. Allah created these forms and then placed that entrusted treasure which is the soul within those forms.

Awwal Muhammad ☉ (A) The emergence of creation; the third of the nine Muhammads ☉.

ayyah (T) Sir; a term of respect.

bā' (A) The Arabic letter (ب) which corresponds to the English consonant 'b'.

Bismillāhir-Rahmānir-Rahīm (A) In the name of God, Most Merciful, Most Compassionate.
　　Bismillāh: Allah, the first and the last; the One with a beginning and without a beginning. He is the One who is the cause for creation and for the absence of creation, the cause for the beginning and for the beginningless. He is the One who is completeness.
　　ar-Rahmān: He is the King, the Compassionate One, and the Beneficent One. He is the One who protects all creations and gives them nourishment. He looks after them, gives them love, takes them unto Himself, and comforts them. He gives them food, houses, property and everything within Himself. He holds His creations within Himself and protects them. He is the One who reigns with justice.
　　ar-Rahīm: He is the One who redeems, the One who protects us from evil, the One who preserves and confers eternal bliss. No matter what we may do, He has the quality of forgiving us and accepting us back. He is the Tolerant One who forgives all the faults we have committed. He is the Savior. On the Day of Judgment, on the Day of Inquiry, and on all days since the beginning, He protects and brings His creations back unto Himself.

chettiyar (T) Merchant.

daulat (A) Wealth; the wealth of Allah's grace. The wealth of Allah is the wealth of divine knowledge *('ilm)* and the wealth of unshakable faith *(īmān).*

dēva (T) Celestial being.

dhikr (A) The remembrance of God. It is a common name given to traditional prayers in praise of God. Of the many *dhikrs,* the most exalted *dhikr* is to say, *"Lā ilāha illallāhu:* There is nothing other than You, O God. Only You are Allah." All the other *dhikrs* relate to His actions *(wilāyats),* but this *dhikr* points to Him and to Him alone. It is the *dhikr* of Allah's *'arsh* (throne). *See also kalimah.*

dīn (A) The pure light; the path of perfect purity. *Dīnul-Islām* is the beauty of the pure light. Perfect purity, its light and its truth are known as *dīn* and *dīnul-Islām.* The resplendence of perfectly pure *īmān,* absolute faith, certitude and determination. Lit. religion; faith; path.

du'ā' (A) A prayer of supplication.

dunyā (A) The earth-world in which we live; the world of physical existence; the darkness which separated from Allah at the time when the light of *Nūr Muhammad* ☉ manifested from within Allah.

fajr (A) The pre-dawn or early morning prayer, the first of the five daily prayers in Islam.

fard (A) Obligatory duty; to understand the rules and commandments of Allah, accept them and act accordingly. In Islam there are five obligatory duties *(furūd)* known as the five pillars: 1. *ash-shahādah* (witnessing that other than God nothing exists and Muhammad is the Messenger of God), 2. prayer, 3. charity, 4. fasting and 5. holy pilgrimage *(hajj).*

Fātihah (A) Opening chapter of the Qur'an; sometimes used to indicate a recitation of the first and last three short chapters of the Qur'an.

fikr (A) Loving contemplation; meditation; concentration on God.

firdaus (A) The eighth heaven. If we can cut away the seven base desires known as the *nafs ammārah,* what remains will be Allah's qualities, actions and conduct, His gracious attributes and His duties. If man can make these his own and store them within his heart, then that is *firdaus.* That is Allah's house of infinite magnitude and perfect purity, a limitless heaven.

Furqān (A) The religion or scripture of Islam, corresponding to the fourth step of spiritual ascendance. Furqān was revealed to Moses ☉ and Muhammad ☉. It is the "criterion" which distinguishes between good and evil, right and wrong, lawful and unlawful, truth and illusion. This is the region of the head and the seven openings (two eyes, two ears, two nostrils and one mouth), through which man receives explanations. *See also* Injīl; Jabrāt; Zabūr.

gnāna guru (T) Teacher; a gnostic with divine wisdom.

gnānam (T) Divine wisdom. If a person can throw away all the worldly wealth and take within him only the treasure called Allah and His qualities and actions, His conduct and behavior, if he makes Allah the only treasure and completeness for him—that is the state of *gnānam*.

gnāni (T) A gnostic; one who has divine wisdom, or *gnānam*, one who has received the qualities and wisdom of God by surrendering to God, and, having received these, lives in a state of peace where he sees all lives as equal.

gul pān (T) A kind of bread.

guru (T) A divinely wise teacher or guide; a sheikh.

hadīth (A) (pl. *ahādīth*) An authenticated account of the acts and words of the Prophet Muhammad ☾; a true account handed down.

hāl (A) A transient state of being or condition of the heart of man which comes without effort.

halāl (A) Permissible; those things that are permissible or lawful according to the commands of God and which conform to the word of God.

Hanal (T) The religion of fire worship; corresponds to the second step of spiritual ascent, *tarīqat* in Arabic, the level at which there is unswerving acceptance of the good. *See also* Jabrāt.

harām (A) That which is forbidden by truth, by justice and by the warnings or commands of God. For those who are on the straight path, *harām* means all the evil things, the actions, the foods and the dangers that can obstruct that path.

hayāt (A) Life; the plenitude of man's eternal life; the splendor of the completeness of life; the soul *(rūh)* of the splendor of man's life.

Hayāt Muhammad ☾ (A) The soul which exists forever; the truth which never dies; the fourth of the nine Muhammads ☾.

hū (A) Within the heart, there is a sound which goes on resonating with the sound, *"Hū, hū, hū, hū!"* It is a resonance which never diminishes no matter how much we take from it. That resonance is *Allāhu. See also* Allah or *Allāhu.*

husnā (A) Inner beauty.

illallāh(u) (A) Nothing other than Allah. The second part of the *dhikr, lā ilāha illallāhu,* which accompanies the breath as it is drawn in through the right nostril and is finally deposited in the inner heart.

īmān (A) Absolute, complete and unshakable faith, certitude and determination that God alone exists; the complete acceptance by the heart that God is One.

Injīl (A) Christianity; corresponds to the third step of spiritual ascent, *haqīqat* in Arabic, the level of the heart at which conversation with God begins. *See also* Furqān; Jabrāt; Zabūr.

insān (A) Man; a human being. The true form of man is the form of Allah's qualities, actions, conduct, behavior and virtues. The one who has realized the completeness of this form, having filled himself with these qualities, is a true *insān.*

'ishā' (A) The night prayer, the fifth of the five daily prayers in Islam.

Jabrāt (A) Fire worship or Zoroastrianism; corresponds to the second level of spiritual ascent, *tarīqat* in Arabic, the level at which there is unswerving acceptance of the good. *See also* Furqān, Hanal, Injīl, Zabūr.

janāzah (A) Funeral prayers.

jinn (A) Subtle beings created out of fire. There are two kinds of jinns. Those formed in bad qualities are called satan's jinns. They do not glorify Allah. They create evil qualities. Those formed within obedience to Allah are different. They are perfectly pure and glorify Allah.

jum'ah (A) In Islam, the Friday congregational prayers held at midday.

kāfir (A) One who conceals Allah's truth; one who fails to live according to Allah's qualities and virtues although being aware of what Allah has commanded and forbidden; one who is ungrateful or who rejects Allah after having awareness of the truth; one who worships things as equal to Allah, falling under the power of his base desires. Such a one hides the truth out of purely selfish motives, turning the heart into the form of darkness, falling prey to the forces of satan and acquiring the qualities of satan.

kalimah (A) The affirmation of faith—*Lā ilāha illallāhu:* There is nothing other than You, O God. Only You are Allah. The *kalimah* is Allah's grace and His pure light of truth, with which we can wash our *qalb,* or inner heart. That is the *awwal kalimah. Awwal* is the time that life appeared. The *kalimah* washes away all the karma that started from the time when each being was created, when each ray appeared and touched the world, resulting in bad qualities or karma. The *kalimah* washes all this away with truth. That is the *awwal kalimah.* This is a small meaning of the *kalimah.* The *kalimah* washes away all the faults and dirt that have been acquired in *awwal,* in the beginning of life. *See also dhikr; subhānallāhi kalimah.*

kangāni (T) Overseer.

karma (T) The inherited qualities formed at the time of conception. After the rays that were in Allah emerged from Him, satan's qualities appeared—the qualities of maya, the qualities of desire, the qualities that are the essence of the five elements, the qualities of the mind, and all the thoughts, looks, and actions that arise from the connection to earth, to hell and to maya. These qualities form karma. What eliminates these from the body is the perfectly pure qualities of *īmān,* Allah's qualities.

karpala (T) Priest.

kasthūri (T) Musk, collected from certain deer, which has medicinal value.

kathpaha virudcham (T) Wish-fulfilling tree.

kiriyai (T) The second step of spiritual ascent in the Hindu tradition.

kitāb (A) Book.

lebbe (U) Person who carries out specific duties in a mosque.

maghrib (A) The evening prayer; the fourth of the five daily prayers in Islam. Lit. sunset.

malā'ikat (A) Bawa Muhaiyaddeen ☺ frequently uses this word to mean the chosen, selected or advanced heavenly beings, referred to as archangels. Lit. angels.

mal'ūn (A) Cursed; rejected; a name given to satan.

mantra (T) An incantation or formula; the recitation of a magic word or set of words; sounds imbued with force or energy through constant repetition, but limited to the energy of the five elements. The *kalimah* is not a mantra.

matham (T) Fanaticism.

maya (T) Illusion; the unreality of the visible world; a hypnotic fascination that arises within the form of darkness; the glitters seen in the darkness of illusion; the one hundred and five million glitters seen in the darkness of the mind which result in one hundred and five million rebirths. Maya is an energy, or *shakthi,* which takes on various shapes, causes man to forfeit his wisdom, and confuses and hypnotizes him into a state of torpor. It can take many, many millions of hypnotic forms. If man tries to grasp one of these forms with his intellect, although he sees the form he will never catch it, for it will elude him by taking on yet another form.

mīm (A) The Arabic letter (م) which corresponds to the English consonant 'm'. In the transformed man of wisdom, *mīm* represents Muhammad ☻. The shape of *mīm* is like a sperm cell and from this comes the *nuqtah*, or dot, which is the form of the world.

mi'rāj (A) The mystical journey of the Prophet Muhammad ☻ through the heavens which took place in the twelfth year of the Prophet's ☻ mission on the twenty-seventh day of the month of *Rajab*. During this event the divine order for the five-times prayer was given. Lit. an ascent.

Muhaiyaddeen ☻ (A) *Mu* is that which is ancient; that which existed earlier; *hayy* is life; *yā* is a title of greatness, a title of praise; and *dīn* means the light of wisdom that is perfectly pure. Thus Muhaiyaddeen ☻ is a treasure that existed from the beginning, the 'ancient thing' that was with God originally and is always with him. It is the pure resplendence called the *Qutb* ☻, the one who reveals the wisdom that lies buried under illusion, revives the life of that wisdom and imparts it to others. It is to that wisdom of purity that God gave the name Muhaiyaddeen ☻. This is the radiant wisdom that manifested from Allah, the wisdom to which He gave His powers *(wilāyats),* the powers arising from His qualities. It is Allah's wondrous radiance that is capable of distinguishing right from wrong. Lit. one who restores to life the path of purity *(dīn);* the reviver of the *dīn. See also Qutb* ☻.

Muhammad ☻ (A) The beauty of the light of Allah's essence present in the heart and reflected in the face. The effulgent face shining with God's light; the brilliant heart of grace; the beauty of the essence of God; the Messenger of Allah; the *Nūr,* the resplendent light of Allah; the beauty of God's qualities, which makes everything in creation rejoice or be blissful.

Muhammad ☻ is the last of the line of prophets. However, he was there from the first, when Allah said, "O Muhammad, I would not have created anything without you." That same beauty, which was present in the beginning, also comes at the end as the beauty of Muhammad ☻.

mu'min (A) A true believer; one of pure faith.

murunga (T) The drumstick tree.

nabī (A) A prophet. One who has accepted Allah's commandments and has surrendered to Him alone is a *nabī.* One who accepts Allah's commandments and covenants and does service to Him, the kind of service which can be rewarded only by Allah is a *nabī.*

nafl (A) Extra prayer.

nafs (A) Person; spirit; inclination; base desires.

nasīb (A) Destiny; fate.

nāyaham (T) Lord or master; noble; a term of profound respect.

nāyan (T) Noble lord.

Nāyan (T) The Lord who protects and sustains.

nuqtah (A) Dot or point; diacritical mark placed over or under certain Arabic letters to differentiate one from the other. The entirety of creation is contained within the *nuqtah* under the Arabic letter *bā'* (ب).

Nūr (A) Light; the resplendence of Allah; the plenitude of the light of Allah which has the brilliance of a hundred million suns; the completeness of Allah's qualities. When the plenitude of all these becomes one and resplends as one, that is the *Nūr*, that is Allah's qualities and His beauty. It is the resplendent wisdom which is innate in man and can be awakened.

Nūr Muhammad ☺ (A) The beauty of the qualities and actions of the powers *(wilāyats)* of Allah, the radiance of Allah's essence *(dhāt)* which shines within the resplendence of His truth. It was the light of Muhammad ☺ called *Nūr Muhammad* ☺ that was impressed upon the forehead of Adam ☺. Of the nine aspects of Muhammad ☺, *Nūr Muhammad* ☺ is that aspect which is Allah's wisdom; the eighth of the nine Muhammads ☺.

pallan (T) A low-caste person.

pūjā (T) Hindu ritual devotion.

Purānas (T) Stories, usually referring to the Hindu scriptures; mythologies; legends; epics. The stories of each religion can be described as Purānas. Some were sent down as commandments from God, others were created through man's intelligence and senses, while still others were created by poets, usually as songs of praise depicting stories.

Qutb ☺ (A) One who functions in the state of divine analytic wisdom *(pahuth arivu)*, the sixth level of consciousness. The one who, having measured the length and breadth of the seven oceans of the base desires, raises up the ship of life that lies buried in the ocean of maya, and rescues it from that ocean of desires. The *qutbiyyat* is the grace, the vibration and the wisdom of Allah's essence that awakens true faith *(īmān)*, restores the twelve weapons of the *Qutb* ☺ from the ocean of maya, and returns the life to the form of purity it had in *arwāh*, when it emerged from Allah. *Qutb* ☺ is also a title used for the great holy men of Islam.

qutbiyyat (A) Divine analytic wisdom, or *pahuth arivu*, which is the sixth level of consciousness; the wisdom of the *Qutb* ☺; the wisdom which explains the truth of God.

Qutbuz-zamān (A) The supreme *Qutb* ☺ of the age.

Rabb (A) The Lord, God; the One who creates everything; the One who awakens everything; the One who manifests all things and then protects them.

Rabbil-'ālamīn (A) The Lord of the universes.

Rahmān (A) The Most Compassionate. *Ar-Rahmān*—one of the ninety-nine beautiful names of Allah *(asmā'ul-husnā)*. The One who rules is forever ruling with His three thousand compassionate, benevolent qualities. He has no anger at all. His duty is only to protect and sustain. *See also Bismillāhir-Rahmānir-Rahīm.*

rahmat (A) God's grace; His mercy; His forgiveness and compassion; His benevolence; His wealth. To all creations, He is the wealth of life *(hayāt)* and the wealth of unshakable faith *(īmān)*. All the good things that we receive from God are His *rahmat*. That is the wealth of God's plenitude. Everything that is within God is *rahmat*, and if He were to give that grace, that would be an undiminishing, limitless wealth

Rahmatul-'ālamīn (A) The mercy and compassion for all the universes; the One who gives everything to all His creations.

rak'at (A) A bowing; to surrender one's heart entirely to God and prostrate to Him. In the five times prayer of Islam, a *rak'at* is one set of a series of motions consisting of standing and bowing, followed by two prostrations.

Rasūl ☺ (A) A messenger, usually referring to the Prophet Muhammad ☺. A *rasūl* is one who accepts God totally, not accepting anything else as God; one who accepts the words and actions of God and acts according to them; one who fulfills God's commandments. The *rasūls* followed the commandments that came down to them, each at their particular time in history.

Rasūlullāh ☺ (A) The Messenger of Allah; a title used for Prophet Muhammad ☺.

rizq (A) Food; sustenance; the single atom of *rahmat* (grace) that comes directly from God as the true nourishment. All the rest of the food—that which comes from the world—is merely hay for man's desires *(nafs)*.

roti (T) A kind of bread.

rūh (A) The soul; the light ray of God; the light of God's wisdom. Bawa Muhaiyaddeen ☺ explains that the *rūh* is life *(hayāt)*. Out of the six kinds of lives it is the light life, the human life. It is a ray of the light of the resplendence of Allah (the *Nūr*), a ray that does not die or disappear. It is the truth. The other five lives appear and disappear. That which exists forever without death is the soul. It is Allah's grace *(rahmat)* which has obtained the wealth of the imperishable treasure of all three worlds *(mubārakāt)*.

rūhānī (A) Elemental spirit arising from desires; the spirit of the elements. There are six kinds of lives within man. One is the human life which is the light life. That is the soul *(rūh).* Associated with this are the lives of earth, fire, water, air and ether. These constitute the *rūhānī.*

rukū' (A) A posture in the daily formal *salāt* (prayer) of Islam, where one bends over from the torso, with head down and hands resting on knees.

rupee (S) The unit of currency in India, Pakistan and Sri Lanka.

sabūr (A) Inner patience. Patience is Allah's treasure chest. Going within this treasure chest, reflecting and having forbearance is *sabūr.*
   Yā Sabūr—one of the ninety-nine names *(asmā'ul-husnā)* of Allah. God, who in a state of limitless patience, is always forgiving the faults of His created beings and continuing to protect them.

sajdah (A) To prostrate oneself in prayer. *Sajdah* is dedicating oneself to the One and handing over one's body, possessions and soul to Him alone. Returning His kingdom, His *qalb* and His truth to Him, surrendering these things to Him alone is *sajdah.* That is *vanakkam,* or worship.

salām (A) Peace; the peace of God. Greetings! When one gives *salāms* to another, it means in God's name or in the presence of God, may both of us become one without any division; both of us are in a state of unity, a state of peace.

salāt (A) Blessing or prayer. Specifically, the prayer that is done five times daily by Muslims.

salawāt (A) (sing. *salāt*) Prayers; blessings; glorification. Giving *salāms* and *salawāt* is the practice of praising, glorifying and invoking Allah, and beseeching peace for the *Rasūl* ⊖, the prophets and the angels and other exalted beings.

sariyai (T) The first step of spiritual ascent in the Hindu tradition.

shaitān (A) Satan; the name given to *iblīs,* the commander of the jinns, after he was condemned by Allah. Satan is born from the fire of anger, jealousy, deceit, arrogance, pride and the egoism of the 'I'; a human being who has these qualities is satan.

shakthi (T) The forces or energies arising from the five elements.

shakūr (A) Gratitude; contentment with whatever may happen, realizing that everything comes from Allah; contentment arising from gratitude; the state within the inner patience known as *sabūr;* that which is stored within the treasure chest of patience.
   Yā Shakūr—one of the ninety-nine beautiful names *(asmā'ul-husnā)* of Allah. To have *shakūr* with the help of the One who is *Yā Shakūr* is true *shakūr.*

shānti (T) True inner peace.

sharī'at (A) The first step of the five steps of spiritual ascendance *(sharī'at, tarīqat, haqīqat, ma'rifat* and *sūfiyyat)*. Since man was created out of the five elements (earth, fire, water, air and ether), since he has within him both light and darkness, good and bad, truth and falsehood and heaven and hell, he must know the good from the bad. Understanding what is right and what is wrong is *sharī'at*. Discarding what is bad and accepting what is good and acting accordingly is *sharī'at*. Lit. the law.

sheikh (A) A spiritual guide or master; one, who knowing himself and God, guides others on the straight path, the path to God.

subhānallāhi kalimah (A) *Subhānallāhi wal-hamdu lillāhi wa lā ilāha illallāhu, wallāhu akbar. Wa lā hawla wa lā quwwata illā billāhi wa huwal-'alīyul-'azīm:* Glory be to God, and all praise is to God, and other than God nothing exists; and Allah is most great, and none has the majesty or the power to sustain except for God, and He is the majesty, the supreme in glory. Also known as *tasbīh,* or the third *kalimah*.

sukūn (A) A diacritical mark in Arabic, denoting a consonant with no vowel sound. Lit. silent; quiet.

sunnah (A) The sayings and practices of the *Rasūl*⊕ or other prophets. Lit. customary.

sūrat (A) Form or shape; with a slightly different spelling in Arabic, also a chapter in the Qur'an.

swami (T) A respectful address; a spiritual master.

tasbīh (A) Glorification of God; offering prayers of praise; purifying the heart, which is the abode of Allah; prayer beads.

tatthwa (T) The strength or power that is inherent in the qualities of the creations, manifesting through the action of each respective quality. While jinns, demons and ghosts have thirty-six *tatthwas,* man has ninety-six, and through these he can control everything.

tawakkul-'alallāh (A) Absolute trust in God; surrender to God; handing over to God the entire responsibility for everything. *Al-Wakīl* is one of the ninety-nine beautiful names of Allah: the Trustee; the Guardian.

thāli (T) Marriage necklace.

thambi (T) Younger brother.

thiru marai (T) The original Qur'an; the inner Qur'an inscribed within the heart.

All the secrets and the essence of the three worlds of *awwal, dunyā* and *ākhirah* (the beginning of creation, the physical world and the realm of God) have been buried and concealed by Allah within the *thiru Qur'ān.* Within it, He has concealed the explanations of the essence of grace *(dhāt)* and of the manifestations of creation *(sifāt).* There He has concealed the *alif, lām* and *mīm;* these three are the essence. That is why it is called the *thiru Qur'ān. Thiru* means triple in Tamil.

Literally, *marai* means holy scriptures, and as such it refers to the scriptures and words of every religion. In this sense it is used to describe the book called the Holy Qur'an. But as Bawa Muhaiyaddeen ⊕ explains, it is the manifestation of the conscience of God in every age to every nation, revealing to mankind the means of attaining Him. This is the inner Qur'an, the original Qur'an, which becomes manifest from time to time, revealing the guidelines of human conduct in relation to spiritual evolution. If God is the reality immanent within man, then the voice of God (the revelation that proceeds from the *Nūr,* the *perr arivu* or divine luminous wisdom) is called *thiru marai.*

'ulamā' (A) (sing. *'ālim*) Teachers; learned ones; scholars.

vadai (T) Spicy bean savory.

wa 'alaikumus-salām (A) May the peace and blessings of Allah be upon you also.

waqt (A) Time of prayer. In the religion of Islam, there are five specified *waqts,* or times of prayer, each day. But truly, there is only one *waqt;* that is the prayer that never ends, wherein one is in direct communication with God and has merged with Him.

wilāyat (A) God's power which has been revealed and manifested through His actions; the miraculous names and actions of God; the powers of His attributes through which all creations came into existence.

yā (A) The vocative 'O!'; an exclamation of praise; a title of greatness or praise.

yōgam (T) The third step of spiritual ascent in the Hindu tradition.

yuga (T) A period of fifty million years in the world's existence. Each cycle of creation consists of four yugas, or two hundred million years. This universe is now nearing the end of the fourth yuga.

Zabūr (A) Corresponds to Hinduism, the first step of spiritual ascent; the creation of forms. *See also* Furqān; Injīl; Jabrāt.

OTHER BOOKS BY
M. R. BAWA MUHAIYADDEEN ⟨رَضِيَ⟩

Truth & Light: brief explanations

Songs of God's Grace

The Divine Luminous Wisdom That Dispels the Darkness

Wisdom of the Divine (Vols. 1–6)

The Guidebook to the True Secret of the Heart (Vols. 1, 2)

God, His Prophets and His Children

Four Steps to Pure Iman

The Wisdom of Man

A Book of God's Love

My Love You My Children: 101 Stories for Children of All Ages

Come to the Secret Garden: Sufi Tales of Wisdom

The Golden Words of a Sufi Sheikh

The Tasty, Economical Cookbook (Vols. 1, 2)

Sheikh and Disciple

Maya Veeram or The Forces of Illusion

Asmā'ul Husnā: The 99 Beautiful Names of Allah

Islam and World Peace: Explanations of a Sufi

A Mystical Journey

Questions of Life—Answers of Wisdom (Vols. 1, 2)

Treasures of the Heart: Sufi Stories for Young Children

To Die Before Death: The Sufi Way of Life

A Song of Muhammad ⊕

Hajj: The Inner Pilgrimage

The Triple Flame: The Inner Secrets of Sufism

*The Resonance of Allah: Resplendent Explanations Arising from
   the Nūr, Allāh's Wisdom of Grace*

Enough for a Million Years

Why Can't I See the Angels: Children's Questions to a Sufi Saint

BOOKLETS

Gems of Wisdom series:
    Vol. 1: The Value of Good Qualities
    Vol. 2: Beyond Mind and Desire
    Vol. 3: The Innermost Heart
    Vol. 4: Come to Prayer

PAMPHLETS

A Contemporary Sufi Speaks:
    To Teenagers and Parents
    On the Signs of Destruction
    On Peace of Mind
    On the True Meaning of Sufism
    On Unity: The Legacy of the Prophets
    The Meaning of Fellowship
    Mind, Desire, and the Billboards of the World

Foreign Language Publications

    Ein Zeitgenössischer Sufi Spricht über Inneren Frieden
    (A Contemporary Sufi Speaks on Peace of Mind—
    German translation)

    Deux Discours tirés du Livre L'Islam et la Paix Mondiale:
    Explications d'un Soufi
    (Two Discourses from the Book, Islam and World Peace:
    Explanations of a Sufi—French translation)

    ¿Quién es Dios? Una explicatión por el Sheikh Sufi
    (Who is God? An Explanation by the Sufi Sheikh—Spanish
    translation)

For free catalog or book information call:
(888) 786-1786
or fax: (215) 879-6307
Web address: http://www.bmf.org

About The
Bawa Muhaiyaddeen Fellowship

Muhammad Raheem Bawa Muhaiyaddeen ☺, a Sufi mystic from Sri Lanka, was a man of extraordinary wisdom and compassion. For over seventy years he shared his knowledge and experience with people of every race and religion and from all walks of life.

The central branch of The Bawa Muhaiyaddeen Fellowship is in Philadelphia, Pennsylvania, which was the home of M. R. Bawa Muhaiyaddeen ☺ when he lived in the United States before his passing in December, 1986. The Fellowship continues to serve as a meeting house, as a reservoir of people and materials for everyone who is interested in his teachings.

The Mosque of Shaikh Muhammad Raheem Bawa Muhaiyaddeen ☺ is located on the same property; here the five daily prayers and Friday congregational prayers are observed. An hour west of the Fellowship is the *Mazār*, the resting place of M. R. Bawa Muhaiyaddeen ☺ which is open daily between sunrise and sunset.

For further information write or phone:

The Bawa Muhaiyaddeen Fellowship
5820 Overbrook Avenue
Philadelphia, Pennsylvania 19131

(215) 879-6300

E-mail address: info@bmf.org
Web address: http://www.bmf.org

If you would like to visit the Fellowship, or to obtain a schedule of current events, branch locations and meetings, please write, phone or e-mail *Attn: Visitor Information.*